TENNIS

About the authors

Dr. Joan Johnson is the women's tennis coach, professor, and associate chairperson of the Department of Physical Education and Athletics at California State University, Los Angeles. She has attended Western Michigan University in Kalamazoo and she received her B.S. degree from the University of Wisconsin. She also attended the University of Michigan and earned the M.S. in Education and Ph.D. degrees at the University of Southern California. She has been selected as United States Women's Tennis Coach for the World University Games and for USTA Junior Wightman Cup teams. She is an experienced tournament competitor, who has traveled throughout the United States, Europe (Wimbledon), and Australia. In addition, Dr. Johnson has directed many tennis coaching clinics and workshops. She is a member of the USTA Women's Collegiate Committee and Southern California Tennis Umpires' Association and was recently appointed chairperson of the Tennis Committee of the Association of Intercollegiate Athletics for Women.

Dr. Johnson is coauthor of *A Workbook for Tests and Measurements in Physical Education* (with David Kelley) and has been elected to serve as president of the Western Society for Physical Education of College Women.

Paul Xanthos is professor of Health, Physical Education, and Recreation, and former chairman of the Health, Physical Education, and Recreation Department for Men at Los Angeles Pierce College. He earned the AB degree at Occidental College in Los Angeles and the MS degree at the University of Southern California. As an undergraduate student-athlete, he participated in intercollegiate track and tennis at Occidental College.

Professor Xanthos has authored *Tennis—A Pictorial Guide for Teachers, Handbook for Tennis Class Organization,* and *Handbook for Conduct and Organization of Tennis Clinics and Teacher Training Workshops,* as well as numerous articles for professional magazines and journals.

As varsity tennis coach at Los Angeles Pierce College, Paul Xanthos has led his players to 7 conference championships in ten years. He has conducted over 200 tennis clinics and teacher workshops throughout the world and is recognized as one of the world's leading exponents of large group instruction. In 1974, he was corecipient of the National Tennis Foundation (USLTA) Award of Merit for his contributions to the development of tennis in the United States. Professor Xanthos is former chairman of the AAHPER/USLTA Joint Committee on Tennis. He is a staff member of both the Lifetime Sports Education Project and the National Tennis Teachers' Conference, a member of the USTA Education and Research Committee, and serves as director of the Tennis Industry Show Educational Program in San Diego.

TENNIS

Physical Education Activities Series

Joan D. Johnson
California State University
Los Angeles

Paul J. Xanthos
Los Angeles Pierce College

THIRD EDITION

Wm C Brown Company Publishers
Dubuque, Iowa

Consulting Editors
    Physical Education
    Aileene Lockhart
    Texas Woman's University

    Parks and Recreation
    David Gray
    California State University, Long Beach

    Health
    Robert Kaplan
    The Ohio State University

Evaluation Materials Editor
    Physical Education Activities
    Jane A. Mott
    Texas Woman's University

Printed in the United States of America   **5/78**

Contents

Preface

Throughout the years, tennis players have developed a wide variety of techniques and styles of play—all designed to outmaneuver the opponent and win the point. That such variety of method exists for the purpose of obtaining but a single objective is silent testimony to the resourcefulness of those who play. Tennis has a rich and fascinating history, both with respect to its past and its continuing development, and also with respect to the interesting personalities who have influenced this development. A thorough study of this aspect of the game would require several volumes and thus is beyond the scope of this publication, but parts of the story are told in the following pages, especially in chapter 8 which contains definitions of the colorful terminology of tennis. In addition, this book presents basic descriptions of tennis skills, some of the underlying reasons which support the descriptions, a condensation and interpretation of the rules as well as the unwritten rules, and a brief discussion of tactics which should be helpful both to the player who wishes to develop his own personalized pattern of play and to the spectator who wishes to become more aware of what is really happening when he watches others play. Other chapters deal with the selection and care of equipment, with tennis organizations, and with suggestions for playing the game.

Self-evaluation questions pertaining to both knowledge and skill are distributed throughout the text. These afford the reader examples of the kinds of understanding and levels of skill that should be acquired as he progresses toward mastery of tennis. Try to respond to these questions thoroughly and competently, and devise additional ones to further stimulate your learning. Since the order in which the content of the text is read and the teaching progression of the instructor are matters of individual decision, the evaluative materials are not necessarily positioned according to the presentation of given topics. In some instances, the student may find that he cannot respond fully and accurately to a question until he has read more extensively or has gained more playing experience. From time to time, he should return to such troublesome questions until he is sure of the answers or has developed the skills called for, as the case may be. Answers to the self-evaluation questions may be found on p. 93.

The authors wish to extend their appreciation to Sue Powell for the illustrations and to Doreen Irish, Peter Holliday, Robert Kramer, Jean Spero, Robert Collins, Sue René, and Yvette Bettar, the models in the photographs.

This third edition attempts to clarify and improve the previous presentations. A new section describes the graduated length method of learning tennis. Enlarged photographs and illustrations should help the learner to visualize text material. Information regarding new developments in tennis equipment and court surfaces is presented along with new sections on World Team Tennis, the growth of the professional prize money circuits and other spectator opportunities. Thorough explanations and examples of the 9 point "sudden death" tie-breaker scoring rules and the no-ad scoring system have been included. The reference list has been expanded to include several new and revised publications that are especially recommended for your information and enjoyment. A comprehensive knowledge test, which the student may find useful in assessing his understanding of tennis, is presented in the appendix. We suggest that you take the test before you read the book, and check your answers against the key on p. 92 to discover your present status.

What tennis is like

1

Tennis is played around the world under the same rules and scoring system: in schools and colleges, on private courts, in public parks, in exclusive clubs, in big cities and small towns, and both indoors and outdoors. It is played on a court 78' long and 36' wide divided by a tautly strung net 3'6" high at the posts but only 3' high in the center (fig. 1.1). Singles is played by two players opposing each other on a narrower court (27' wide); when four players play, two on one side opposing two on the other, the game is called doubles. Each player uses a racket, usually made of several laminations of wood strung with nylon or gut, to hit a rubber, felt-covered ball back and forth across the net, within the boundaries of the court.

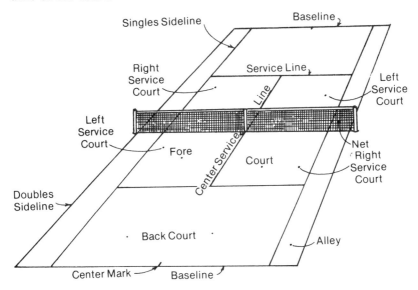

Fig. 1.1   Diagram of the Court

Rules of the game impose some highly specific conditions upon the players, but the general idea is to hit the ball into your opponent's court in such a way that your opponent is unable to return it to your court or that the ball is returned so weakly that you can surely "put it away" with your next shot. This may sound as though points are decided by one or two shots, and, while this does happen in contests between "big game" stylists, usually it takes many more shots to maneuver your opponent out of position, especially when the opponent is trying to do the same thing to you.

The game is started when one player, standing behind his own baseline to the right of the center mark, tosses the ball up and serves to the opponent. The serve must go over the net and must land in the diagonally opposite right service court. If the first serve is unsuccessful, the server has another chance. If that, too, is a fault, the receiver wins the point. The second point is started from the left of the center mark and the serve is directed to the left service court. The third point is started as the first, in the right court, and so on until the game is over. If a serve is good, the receiver attempts to return the ball anywhere into the opponent's court. The rally continues until one player hits the ball into the net or outside the opponent's court boundaries or lets the ball bounce twice in his court, in which case he loses the point. The served ball *must bounce* in the proper service court, but after the serve, a player may elect to move in toward the net to hit the ball before it bounces and make a shot called a volley. If one player has advanced to the net, the opponent may try to lob the ball over the head of the net player; if the lob is too short to be truly effective, the net player may be able to reach up and smash it back into the opponent's court. At the end of the first game, the server becomes the receiver and vice versa; players alternate thus throughout the match. A player must win at least four points to win a game, at least six games to win a set, and at least two sets to win a match.

Similarities between the skills of tennis and the skills of other games will be noticed by the discerning reader. For example, the ready position and footwork in tennis is often compared with that of basketball. The tennis two-step may also be found on a dance floor. The sidearm movement pattern used to hit most groundstrokes is similar to that used by the baseball batter. The overhead swing of the tennis serve and smash contains many of the same elements as the badminton clear and smash, the overhand pitch in baseball, and the volleyball overhand serve. Volleying in tennis has been likened to the boxer's jab and to the reaching movement used to catch a ball out in front. Other comparisons could be made, but these will be left to the reader.

VALUES

All kinds of people play tennis, and they play for many reasons. Tennis can truly be called the sport of a lifetime, since youngsters can begin at about six years of age and their grandparents may still be playing even past age sixty! Young and old, men and women, highly skilled champions and eager neophytes, all express their enthusiasm for the game both on and off the court. Execution of the strokes demands coordination and skill, fine timing of racket, arm, body, and feet. Stamina and endurance are required to persist through long rallies and matches, but healthy exercise is provided for all, even at the moderate pace of intermediate players. The challenge of outwitting the opponent exists at all levels of skill and many a match has been won by the lesser skilled player through the application of superior tactics. Understanding one's strengths in order to exploit the opponent's weaknesses demands keen analysis and quick anticipation. It requires self-discipline to practice purposefully and self-control to persist throughout the sometimes trying conditions of match play. Raising one's game to meet the demands of competition can produce a most satisfying feeling. Finally, tennis provides a marvelous social situation. Only one other person is necessary to play, but many people all over the world do play, and the friendly spirit inherent in the words, "Would you like to hit some?" or, as the English say, "Let's have a knock, shall we?" is all the introduction you need. Issue this invitation yourself, and you'll soon see what fun it is!

COURTS

Courts come in a variety of surfaces and surroundings. While the official rules specify the dimensions of the court, the height and location of the net posts, the width of the lines, and the like, nothing is said about the court surface. Of course, the world's official governing body, the International Lawn Tennis Federation, does have the word "lawn" in its title! Nevertheless, in addition to grass, clay, concrete, asphalt, wood, linoleum, cork, and several other types of surfaces are currently used. The USTA lists approximately 100 brands of court surfaces, and as the popular interest in tennis continues to grow, so does the list. The five major categories of court surfaces are listed below.

   1.   Grass courts, the original surface for "lawn tennis," provide an easy surface for your feet, produce a low-bouncing ball, demand costly maintenance procedures, and do not withstand heavy usage.

   2.   Clay-type courts, those with a loose, granular surface, permit players to slide into their shots, produce a high-bouncing ball, and require careful use and extensive maintenance.

   3.   Hard courts, usually concrete or asphalt with a colorful painted top surface, are hard on your feet and legs, produce a medium high bounce, and demand very little in the way of maintenance.

   4.   The new cushioned courts, which add a resilient layer of material to a concrete or asphalt base, are very expensive to install but provide a comfortable sponginess underfoot, produce a high, slow bounce similar to clay, and are relatively easy to maintain.

   5.   The synthetic, artificial surfaces will most likely be seen while you're watching the pros play in an indoor arena. These textile and plastic carpets can be placed on top of almost any surface. Some are suitable for outdoor use and playing characteristics vary.

   Most tennis experts agree that the surface influences, to a considerable degree, the type of rebound and thus the effectiveness of various strokes, strategies, and styles of play. A beginner could probably care less about the court surface, but as you gain in skill and experience, and venture forth to a variety of playing sites, you will be able to enjoy your game better if you are aware of

---

Holding your racket with the "choked grip" (the hand near the throat of the racket), can you tap the ball to the ground so it will bounce approximately waist-high 50 times in succession? Keep your left foot in place. Can you tap the ball into the air 50 times without allowing it to fall to the ground? Do the flip drill keeping the ball in play by tapping it into the air with alternate sides of the racket face. See how many taps you can get in one minute.

---

the differences in court surfaces. Take the time to adjust your timing and footwork to the bounce of the ball and the speed of the play. Whatever the surface, before you play, see that the court is safe. Remove loose dirt, leaves, glass, or other dangerous objects on which you might slip or fall, and close the gates to prevent running into one unexpectedly left open. (This also prevents much unnecessary ball chasing.)

DRESS

Rubber-soled canvas or leather tennis shoes with good support will provide you with effective footwear necessary for quick starts and stops. Two pairs of socks, the inner pair of cotton and the outer pair of wool, help to prevent blisters and also help to cushion the shock of sudden starts and stops, especially when worn inside tennis shoes that must fit well. A proper fit in socks is important. A size too large is no better than one too small.

Fashionable colored tennis apparel is becoming increasingly popular and more readily available. The traditional white tennis attire reflects heat better than other colors, especially bright or dark colors, so white is the best color to wear on a hot sunny day. It is most important to wear clothing that is comfortable and that provides for the freedom of movement demanded by the game. Top tournament players are extremely conscious of their appearance. They wear clean, well-pressed, attractive clothing and present a neat, well-groomed appearance on the court. You too can appear on the court looking like a tennis player; this will help you to become a better one!

Generally, men wear T-shirts or cotton knit shirts with collars and cotton or Terylene shorts. Women wear a feminine version of the knit shirt either with shorts or with tennis skirts. Modern, drip-dry, nonwrinkle fabrics have greatly simplified caring for tennis clothing. Even though such fabrics increase the cost of the garment, the durability and ease of care make this type of shorts and skirts highly desirable. Many women wear tennis dresses made of various materials and potential Wimbledon champions may have dresses designed especially for them by leading tennis fashion designers. Some girls design and sew their own dresses, making them plain or frilly to suit individual tastes. The keynote in all designs, however, is comfort, freedom of action, and ease of care.

Some players wear wristbands or wristlets made of an absorbent, slightly elasticized material which helps to keep perspiration from the hands. All players should have some type of sweater or jacket to put on after playing to prevent too rapid cooling off or stiffening muscles. The material and weight of the sweater or jacket depends upon playing conditions (for example, the amount of wind, the temperature, general weather), and while white is still a popular color, other colors are acceptable and are frequently used. In addition, caps, assorted styles of floppy hats, sunshades, headbands, towels, and other gear are used by individual players for a variety of reasons. However, you do not need to spend all your money on apparel; you will look right in inexpensive, neat tennis clothing.

BALLS

The official United States Tennis Association rules provide a complete, detailed description of an acceptable tennis ball, and the exact manner in which certain tests must be made is specified. The ordinary player needs to know only that most balls are made of molded rubber, covered with a fuzzy wool felt, and inflated with compressed air for resilience. So-called heavy-duty balls are covered with extra felt which increases their durability. Some balls are now made without the compressed air center and achieve resilience from their rubber centers. Players may choose from a variety of colors, including white, orange, fuschia and optic yellow. Many claim that the brighter colors enhance their ability to see the ball sooner. Optic yellow seems to be the most popular among the better players. Balls stamped with USTA approval meet the rule specifications at the time of packaging but will not retain these qualities indefinitely. In order to maintain the air pressure within the ball, balls are packaged in pressurized cans which should not be opened until the balls will be used in order to prevent loss of pressure or "dead" balls. The heavy-duty ball or the nonpressurized ball is probably the best buy for a beginner, since most experts recommend learning the game with "heavy" balls, that is, with balls which have retained their original weight and have not become light as a result of wearing down the felt cover until only the skin is left. Skinned balls are impossible to control effectively and frequently force beginners, who try to economize on balls, into bad stroke habits. New balls are the only ones with a dependable bounce. In most tournaments, new balls are put into play every nine or eleven games. Both beginners and champions benefit from dependable bounces. Give the skinless wonders to the dog, and give yourself a chance to get started on the right track toward a lifetime of enjoyable tennis!

RACKETS

The rules, which are so specific about the ball, say nothing about the racket. Thus, it would be legal for you to play with any implement you desire—a broom, a frying pan, a solid paddle, a baseball bat, anything! The wonder of it all is that, with no official requirement, tennis rackets are so uniform in dimension (27" long and 9" wide across the face) that two rackets can be used to measure the height of the net at its center (36"). Figure 1.2 shows top-quality rackets with the important parts labeled.

Of course, some companies have experimented with racket variations. One manufacturer produced a racket that was 28" long and advertised the advantages of "the big inch." Another variation has the standard size racket head but a

Fig. 1.2   Parts of the Racket

shorter handle; this reduces the length of the lever and facilitates control but lessens speed; it is especially useful for children and beginners. Players who produce their strokes with two hands on the racket have usually increased the length of the leather grip on the handle. One newly produced racket has an oversized head, another a tear-drop shape, and still another is strung with a new and different pattern of stringing.

In addition to these rather unusual variations, the standard size racket is customarily produced with variations in the type of wood used, number of laminations, weight, balance, grip size, and, of course, cost. The most recent innovations in tennis equipment are the new metal, combination metal and wood, and fiberglass rackets.

Selection and care of equipment are presented more completely in a later chapter. For now, on with the game! Look again at Figure 1.2. You should be able to identify the various parts of the racket so that the descriptions of the basic strokes in the next chapter will be as clear as possible.

Skills essential for everyone

2

Before a child can walk, he must learn to crawl, and before he can run, he must learn to walk. Before he is able to employ the serve, the volley, the ground-strokes, the speed, the placements of the "big game" of a champion, the neophyte must begin from the beginning and establish a sound foundation for his future game. Jimmy Connors, Billie Jean King, Rod Laver, Margaret Court, Arthur Ashe, Evonne Goolagong, Pancho Gonzalez, and Chris Evert didn't walk onto the tournament court without first spending countless hours on the practice court. Follow their example. Learn to grip your racket properly for the variety of strokes you will be called upon to make. Learn the basic waiting or ready position from which you will initiate a number of groundstrokes and volleys. Learn the footwork that will quickly propel you to the best position from which to execute your return. When you do, you will be well on your way to enjoying a lifetime of tennis.

This chapter will provide a framework of sound tennis fundamentals. Keep in mind that, within this framework, there is a certain amount of flexibility, a certain "range of correctness." There is no "only way" to hold your racket, no exact length of backswing, no perfect point of impact. A slight turn of the hand on the grip, a shorter or longer backswing, meeting the ball a little sooner or later may produce the desired results. However, start with the directions as they are presented. If these don't produce the results you want, experiment a little. But stay within the reasonable limits of the "range." The directions are presented for right-handed players; left-handed players will need to reverse them.

THE READY POSITION

Tennis, like most sports, finds one side on the offensive and the other on the defensive. The stance assumed by the player on defense is one of readiness. It is the position from which the player is ready to move quickly forward, back, side to side, and diagonally forward and back. Whether waiting for the serve or in the center of the baseline, the stance is similar. Slight variations are made on an individual basis, often depending upon the abilities of both the player and the opponent. The initial position in singles is approximately three feet behind the baseline in the center of the court. This is the position to which you will return after most baseline shots. Consider the following points when assuming the ready position (fig. 2.2):

1. Face your opponent, feet comfortably spread, knees slightly bent (locked knees must be unlocked before quick movement can take place), body relaxed, and weight slightly forward.
2. Hold your racket in front of you, the throat resting on the fingertips of your left hand, left thumb on top. Hold the racket handle firmly in the right hand with the forehand grip so that the racket head is slightly higher than the handle.
3. Point the head of your racket in the direction of your opponent, the end of the handle close enough to your waist to make the position comfortable without tension.

THE FOREHAND DRIVE

The forehand drive, or stroke, is used to contact a ball on the right of the player. The stroker turns to face the right sideline with his left side pointing toward the net with the forward foot, shoulder, and hip directed toward the shot. As the ball is contacted, the palm of the hand and the forearm move in the direction of the net. The forehand is the fundamental stroke, and many say it is the most important. Without a backhand or a volley, it is possible to play tennis somewhat awkwardly, but without a forehand, it is almost impossible to play at all. For nine out of ten players, the forehand is the side from which the attacking stroke mainly comes.

Grip

Several grips are used by the more advanced players and professionals, but most of these are only slight variations of the grip here described. This material will confine the preliminary instruction to what will be referred to only as the "forehand grip." As you become more advanced, you may make slight adjustments and variations to suit your individual preferences. For now, follow these instructions, referring to the photographs for clarification (fig. 2.1).

Fig. 2.1 Forehand Grip

1. Rest the throat of your racket on the fingertips of your left hand. The face of the racket is perpendicular to the ground with the racket pointing to the net and the butt about six inches from your waist.
2. Place the palm of your hand against the back of the grip so the palm and face of the racket are both in the same plane.
3. Close your hand and "shake hands with your racket." The grip is firm enough for control but not too tight or rigid. *Spread the fingers*, making certain that the index finger is apart from the middle finger and is bent to form a "trigger finger." Wrap the thumb around the grip until it touches the middle finger. The first knuckle of the index finger is on the top right bevel of the grip; the **V** formed by the thumb and index finger is in the center of the top plate.

With this grip, the face of your racket becomes an extension of the palm of your hand. Hold the racket with this grip; turn your hand and wrist over and under, and note that the face of the racket makes similar changes. Make a final adjustment of your hand on the grip so that it feels right. You have now taken the first step in learning the forehand drive. This grip may feel strange at first, and you may develop the tendency to shift your grip to the right and under the

Fig. 2.2   Forehand Drive

Ready Position	Backswing: Turn	Backswing: Step

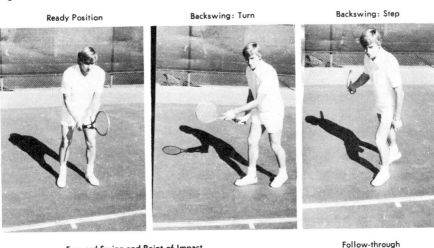

Forward Swing and Point of Impact   Follow-through handle. Periodically, go over the description and make any necessary corrections to return to your original grip.

Backswing

The movement begins as soon as the ball leaves your opponent's racket and you have sensed its direction. The speed with which your racket is drawn back depends upon the speed of the oncoming ball. With practice, you will be able to time the backswing so that the ensuing forward movement occurs without a hitch or pause in the stroke. The racket is taken back at the height of the approaching ball: If it is shoulder high, bring the racket back shoulder high; if waist high, bring the racket back waist high; if knee high, *bend your knees* in order to bring the racket back in line with the oncoming ball.

The backswing consists of two definite movements, the *turn* and the *step*.

Turn

1. From the ready position, begin the backswing by pushing the throat of the racket toward the right sideline with the fingers of your left hand. This will bring your hips and shoulders to the side-to-net or stroking position. The backswing may be initiated either with the left hand pushing the racket or with the shoulders turning to start the arms and racket in motion.
2. As you make the turn, pivot on the heel of your back foot and the ball of the left foot, while shifting the weight to the back foot.
3. As the movement is being completed, head, eyes, side, and shoulder face the net while the racket still points straight ahead (toward the sideline) in its original position (in relation to the body).

Step   The backswing is continued and completed with the combined step and movement of the racket.

1. Move your forward foot in the direction of the ball, and, at the same time, continue the backswing of the racket until it has reached a position slightly lower than the hip, pointing straight back to the back fence. The long strings remain parallel to the ground. The head of the racket is even with or slightly higher than the wrist. The face is slightly open (fig. 2.3).

Fig. 2.3   Closed, Flat or Square, and Open Racket Faces

2. Your weight is over the back foot, which is parallel to the net, while the forward foot points toward the right net post. The knees are flexed.

3. Extend your left arm slightly away from the body using it as a counterbalance.

4. The upper arm and elbow of the racket hand stay close to your right side and hip, with the elbow bent slightly. "Breaking" your wrist slightly will provide a snap to the stroke during the drive through the ball.

Forward Swing

This is the movement of the racket as it moves forward to intercept the flight of the ball at the point of impact. It will vary with the height of the oncoming ball as well as with the position in its trajectory (for example, on the rise, at the top, or as it is coming down—fig. 2.4), at which impact will occur. This description of the forward swing is based on the supposition that the ball has started to drop (after the bounce), and the goal is to make contact at waist level.

1. Adjust the face of the racket so that it is behind and slightly below the expected point of impact. A slight bend of the knees may help to keep the racket parallel to the ground.

2. Shift your weight forward toward the ball by pushing from the back foot and bending the lead knee. At the same time, rotate your hips and shoulders forward.

3. As your weight shifts forward and your body pivots, swing your racket forward and upward, wrist firm and slightly bent back, elbow away from the body, and arm comfortably extended. A slight, controlled forward movement of the wrist helps to bring the hand forward. Keep the racket head even with or slightly above wrist level.

4. The forward swing is fast enough to cause the racket head to "swish" through the air. Continue the stroke through the point of impact toward your intended target. Keep the face of the racket "square" to the ball as long as possible.

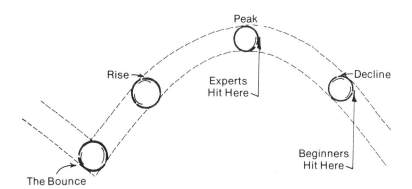

Fig. 2.4   Rise, Top, and Descent After Bounce

Can you do the ball drop and hit drill (forehand and backhand)? Start with your side toward the net, drop the ball with your left hand and stroke it over the net or against a backboard or fence; later, start from the ready position. Can you hit 10 good drives in succession? 15? 20? What is a "good" drive?

5. The point of impact for the forehand grip presented is opposite the left foot. Watch the ball closely throughout the stroke, and see it hit the strings of your racket. Keep your grip and wrist firm at impact.

Follow-through and Finish

The follow-through is the continuation of the forward swing through the ball in the direction of the intended target. A poor follow-through will often negate the preparation prior to the point of impact. A good follow-through will assure both power and direction. Beginners tend to stop the swing when the racket contacts the ball. To aid in insuring a good follow-through and in making a good finish:

1. Continue the forward swing *through the ball* in the direction of the intended target.
2. Finish the stroke with the racket standing on edge pointing up to the top of the opposite fence.
3. Reach as far as you can toward your target, and finish with your hand in front of and slightly higher than your left shoulder.
4. Complete your turn so that you are facing the net, shoulders and hips released by lifting the back heel and pivoting on the toe.
5. Most of your weight is now on the forward foot. Check this by seeing whether you can lift your back foot. The forward knee is bent slightly to help maintain balance and to facilitate a quick return to the ready position.
6. As you complete your turn, resume the hold on the throat of the racket with the left hand and return to the *ready position* for the next shot.

THE BACKHAND DRIVE

While the forehand drive may be considered the "bread-and-butter" stroke of the majority of players, none can expect to achieve any great degree of success without also mastering the backhand drive. A correctly executed backhand presents a picture of smoothness and coordination as the racket moves in the direction of the target without restriction. Balls hit far to your left must be returned with a backhand stroke because you can't get into position for a forehand. There is little time, and it would take too much energy to run around every ball driven to your court in order to make a forehand return. One alternative is to hit with your left hand, which would require practice in achieving that skill. Learning to hit the backhand is quicker and easier!

There are only a few basic differences between the forehand and the backhand drives. Most of the same principles apply. Study the directions well, note the comparisons, and apply the principles. Before long, you may find the backhand a friend, rather than a shot to avoid. Properly hit, it is just as effective as the forehand. Although, like the forehand, the backhand is a fluid, continuous motion when properly executed, it will be presented in its separate parts.

Grip

The following cues will assist you in making the change from the forehand to the backhand grip (fig. 2.5).

1. With the racket held by the fingers of your left hand and with the face of the racket perpendicular to the ground, turn your right hand and wrist on the grip so that the hand moves on top of the grip with the palm facing the top plate.
2. Close your hand on the grip and see that the first knuckle of the index finger is on the center of the top plate. The **V** formed by the thumb and index finger is on the top left bevel of the grip, and the thumb is diagonally across the back of the grip. Later, you may want to wrap the thumb around the grip. The *fingers are spread slightly*, with pressure exerted by the last three fingers.

Fig. 2.5   Backhand Grip

Change from the forehand to the backhand grip is made simultaneously with the beginning of the backswing and must be practiced until it becomes automatic. And remember, relax the grip between shots to avoid tiring the hand and arm.

Backswing

Turning on the backhand is more pronounced than on the forehand, and the body, at the completion of the backswing, is coiled like a steel spring. With the right hip toward the net, the arm and racket move to a position behind the body. The arm and racket, of necessity, are closer to the body than in the forehand.

Turn

1. From the ready position, the racket is pulled back with the fingers of the left hand. The left arm remains almost straight.
2. The grip change is made by holding the racket with the fingers of the left hand while the right hand takes the backhand grip. Skilled players may simply move the right hand on the handle without using the left hand at all.
3. The shoulders and hips turn, and the weight shifts to the back foot.

Step

1. As the backswing continues, the forward foot steps across so that the back is half turned toward the net and the toes of the foot point in the direction of the left net post. The stance is slightly closed, more so than for the forehand.
2. The weight is over the back foot, and the right shoulder is even with or slightly lower than the left. This is aided by bending the forward knee.
3. The right arm hangs down from the shoulder, and the elbow is *slightly* bent with the thumb opposite and a few inches from the left hip. The racket face is slightly open.
4. The head and eyes are watching the flight of the ball *over the forward shoulder*, while the back of the shoulder faces the net.

Forward Swing

Following the turn, the racket is moved forward, directly into the ball. On contact, for a waist-high ball, the face of the racket is almost square to the ball. The face is opened slightly for balls lower than the waist in order to lift the ball up and over the net. As the forward swing begins:

1. The head of the racket is raised or lowered to a suitable position for hitting through the ball.
2. The weight is shifted forward by pushing from the back foot and bending the forward knee.
3. The uncoiling of the hips and shoulders initiates the forward swing of the racket.
4. The hand and racket move away from the hip in the direction of the ball. The right arm is straightened and brought around the body. The racket head picks up speed (listen for the "swish") as the wrist and elbow straighten. The racket head continues its path into and through the ball.
5. Just before impact, the grip tightens on the racket. The ball is contacted six to twelve inches in front of the forward foot. Watch the ball until after your racket has contacted it.

Follow-through and Finish

As in the forehand, a good follow-through is necessary to impart power and direction to the ball. Do not make the mistake of stopping your swing the instant you contact the ball.

Ready Position   Backswing: Turn   Backswing: Step

Forward Swing and Point of Impact   Follow-through

Fig. 2.6   Backhand Drive

1. The racket head continues *through the ball* in the direction of the target area.
2. The arm, wrist, hand, and racket form a straight line, and the racket stands on edge.
3. At the finish, the hand is at shoulder level or slightly higher. The left arm acts as a counterbalance, remaining below the racket arm.
4. The body turn is completed as the body faces the net. The hips and shoulders are square to the net.
5. The weight is on the forward foot, and the forward knee is bent slightly, not stiff or locked.
6. When the stroke has been completed, return quickly to the ready position, ready for the next shot.

FOOTWORK

Since the ball will rarely come to you in perfect position to be hit, you must move into position to hit the ball. Footwork is one of the most important fundamentals of tennis. Good footwork gets you into the best possible position from which to execute your shots and greatly facilitates this execution, while poor footwork causes you to hit from awkward, off-balance positions, making easy shots more difficult and hard shots almost impossible. The following basic suggestions will be helpful in improving your footwork.

1. When waiting for the return, assume a good ready position.

2. As soon as you determine the direction of the ball, push off quickly with the left foot for a ball going to your right and with the right foot when going to your left. Pushing off the balls of the feet contributes to a faster start.

3. Approach the ball with normal running strides as far as possible, lengthening them or shortening them depending upon the amount of ground to be covered. Take large steps first, then smaller steps, and make your final adjustment by using a little skip or two-step.

4. For balls close to you, skip or slide into position, moving the near foot in the direction of the movement first, then bringing the other foot up to it.

5. Stop *just before* reaching a point behind where the ball will bounce. In catching a ball, a player would position himself directly behind the oncoming throw, but in striking a tennis ball, the length of the racket permits you to be to one side of the oncoming ball, much like a baseball batter stands beside home plate instead of directly on or behind it.

6. Prepare for the stroke as you run for the ball, moving the racket part way around while running and completing the backswing with the setting of the feet for the shot. *Play your shot from the side-to-net position whenever possible.*

7. Immediately after executing the stroke, return to the position of readiness.

THE SERVE

The serve is the stroke that puts the ball in play. It has become the principal weapon of attack and is used to place the opponent on the defensive by forcing him to play from his weak side as well as by moving him out of position. A strong serve bolsters an otherwise weak game and tends to build the server's confidence.

Because both hands are in motion at the same time (ball toss and racket arm), coordination may often be difficult for the beginner. To a point, serving is like throwing a baseball overhand; however, in addition to the throwing motion, the placement of the ball in the hitting position (ball toss) introduces another element. The serve requires the coordination of these two movements to bring the ball and racket into position for the most effective contact.

Grip

The grip that is taught to beginners by most teachers and tennis professionals is the forehand grip. However, it is advisable to move to the conventional service grip, halfway between the forehand and backhand, as soon as possible. Some beginners may be able to begin with this service grip which is more flexible and can be used for several types of serves, including the slice, top, twist, and flat serves (fig. 2.7). In the service grip, the **V** formed by the thumb and fore-

Fig. 2.7   Serve Grip and
Ball Hold

finger lies on the line between the top plate of the grip and the top left bevel.
The fingers are spread and the thumb is wrapped around the handle. The grip
is firm but not tight. Clutching the grip too tightly restricts wrist action which
is necessary in serving.

Stance

Take a position three or four feet from the center mark. The left foot is two
or three inches behind the baseline, the toes pointing toward the right net post.
The back foot is perpendicular to the point of aim, about 18" or a comfortable
pace behind the front foot. An extension of a line drawn from toe to toe should
point to the target.

The racket is cradled at its throat in the left hand with the right elbow
close to the body. The racket head is tilted up and points in the direction of
the serve. One or two balls are held in the fingers of the left hand. The weight is
on the back foot, both knees are slightly bent, and the entire body is poised but
not tense. Relaxation and balance are extremely important.

Keep the toes of the left foot in contact with the ground throughout the
serve, moving it only after contact has been made and the momentum of the
racket pulls you into the court. Keeping the foot on the ground will give you a
firm base from which to hit and at the same time will eliminate possible foot
faults.

Ball Toss

Balls are held in the fingers of the left hand, palm up. The ball to be tossed is
held by the thumb, index, and middle fingers. The second ball is held against
the heel of the hand by the fourth and fifth fingers. The ball is "placed" in the
air (not thrown) by an extension of the arm and hand, beginning at the waist
and ending in full extension forward of the right shoulder. The ball should be
tossed with little or no spin. The proper height for the toss may be determined
by extending the arm and racket to the point of impact. The ball should be
tossed slightly higher than the racket strings.

For the flat serve, the ball is tossed *in front of the right shoulder*, and the
ball is hit on the nose; for a slice serve, the ball is tossed to the right and the

Fig. 2.8 Ball Toss
and Racket Face Angle
for Three Types of Serves:
American Twist, Slice, Flat

racket hits the "right eye" of the ball; and for a twist serve, the ball is tossed over the player's head and is hit on the "left eye," the racket starting behind and to the left of the ball (fig. 2.8). Whatever the type of serve, it is essential that the toss be consistent if the serve is to be effective. According to rule, you don't have to swing at a bad toss.

The serve, like the groundstrokes, is presented one step at a time. The grip, stance, and ball toss have been briefly described. Of equal and perhaps more importance is the action of the serving arm, the actual "weapon." The first movement, coordinated with the ball toss, is the *backswing*, the downward-upward or drawing action of the arm and racket; second, the *forward swing* and upward snap into the point of contact; and finally, the *follow-through and finish*.

Backswing

As the ball toss begins, the right arm and racket begin the downward swing with the edge of the racket leading. The left and right arms move downward and upward in unison (down together—up together). The ball is released just before the left arm reaches full extension. The racket head begins an arc that starts in front of the body, continues backward and upward behind the body to a position head high with the wrist in an uncocked position (like the wind-up of an overhead throw). Then the elbow and the wrist start to break, allowing the racket head to drop behind the back until the racket head points straight down to the ground. The trunk and shoulders have rotated away from the net. At this time, the ball has reached the peak of its height.

Forward Swing

As the ball starts down, the weight shifts forward, the trunk and shoulders rotate forward, and the wrist and elbow snap the racket head upward and forward, contacting the ball with body, arm, and racket at full extension, the top of the racket head angled forward (closed) slightly. The movement described here

Fig. 2.9   The Serve

is similar to that of throwing a ball across the net with an overhand motion. The ball is struck just as it starts to drop, and the racket should be moving so rapidly that you can hear it "swish" through the air. The body should not "jackknife" or bend sharply at the waist before or during the serve.

Follow-through and Finish

The follow-through is *out* (not down) in the direction of ball flight and is a natural continuation of the stroke. It continues with the head of the racket swinging freely past the left side of the body. The right foot crosses the baseline and continues forward, taking a step in the direction of the serve to help maintain balance. In the future, this step will become the basis of your approach to the net.

THE VOLLEY

Although it is not necessary to be able to volley to play tennis, lack of volleying ability will limit the offensive potential of a player. At some time or another, he will find himself at net with the opportunity to volley the return for a winner. Doubles play is built around the serve and volley, and volleying is definitely a part of the "big game" that is the trademark of today's champions.

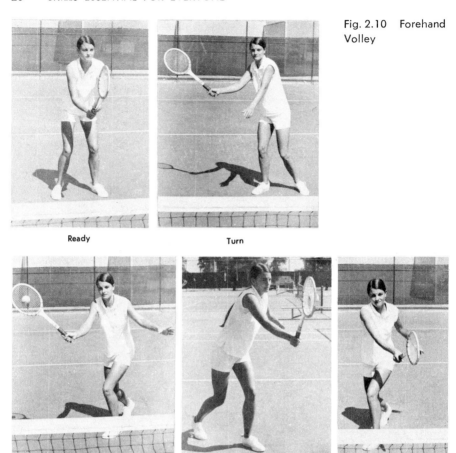

Fig. 2.10   Forehand Volley

Ready	Turn

Hit	Contact Well in Front	Finish

The volley, an abbreviated stroke, is taken in the air before the ball bounces, usually from a position near the net. To be effective, it is made above net height where it can be hit downward for a winner. If the ball is contacted below the level of the net, the volley becomes a defensive shot and must be hit up to clear the net. This may set it up for your opponent who is waiting for the high ball that he can put away for a winner. The volley movement is more of a punch or block than the longer sweep of the groundstroke. Since both forehand and backhand volleys are very similar, they are discussed here simultaneously.

Grip

The grips are the same as those used for the forehand and backhand groundstrokes. In the high backhand volley, the thumb is sometimes moved up the handle to brace the racket against the impact of the ball. Some players use the same grip for both volleys. This grip is halfway between the forehand and backhand grips described previously and is very similar to the service grip.

Stance

The basic volleying position is about six to eight feet away from the net. The ready position is the same as for the groundstrokes, except that the head of the racket is held slightly higher, approximately at eye level. This keeps the volleyer's racket in position to make a quick backswing in preparation for either a forehand or a backhand volley.

Backswing

There is little or no backswing in most volleys; in general, the shorter, the better, especially for the punch volley. The head of the racket should be visible out of the corner of the eye at the end of the backswing. However, for a ball approaching slowly (a soft return), it may be necessary to increase the length of the backswing to gain added power. For a ball approaching rapidly, the backswing may be no more than a slight turn of the shoulders. Usually, the shoulder turn is combined with a step toward the ball with the lead foot (left foot for forehand volleys, right foot for backhand volleys). For a ball approaching at shoulder height, the head of the racket is halfway between the horizontal and vertical position. As the racket is pulled back, bend the wrist back slightly and lock it to eliminate movement on the forward swing. Pull the racket back to a position behind the spot where you intend to meet the ball.

For the backhand, the grip is changed during the backswing and the racket is guided back with both hands. The left hand is released at the beginning of the forward swing. Take the racket back by bending the left elbow, thus lifting the racket head above the wrist and the approaching ball. As in the backhand drive, skilled players may simply move the right hand on the grip without using the left hand at all.

Forward Swing

Use an arm and shoulder motion to move the racket head forward and into the ball. The forward knee is bent with the forward step to provide for the shift of weight. The ball is contacted *well out in front of the body*. The ball is met with a firm tap or punch, the wrist remaining firm on contact.

Follow-through and Finish

There is a slight follow-through in the direction of the placement. Limit the extent of the volley so that a blocking or punching motion is used, and a very short follow-through will result. Return to the ready position immediately, pulling the elbows back to their original position.

For a ball hit directly to you, the backhand volley is used and becomes a protective shot. It is accomplished by shifting the elbow to the right and dropping the racket head into a horizontal position in front of the body. The backswing, of course, will be limited by the body, and the volley stroke itself can only be a short punch or block. For balls hit slightly to the right of center, the

Ready   Turn   Hit

Fig. 2.11   Backhand Volley

Finish

volleyer leans to the left and makes a forehand volley. The reverse holds true for balls hit to the left of center.

Although there is reference to a flat volley in the preceding description, most volleys impart a slight backspin to the ball. This is produced by starting above the ball and hitting forward and slightly downward behind it. Balls hit from below the level of the net must be hit with an open face and a slight lifting motion.

Better players master these strokes

3

At some stage in your progress, you will want to begin experimenting with and developing what are often referred to as auxiliary strokes. These are variations of the basic strokes and are used by more advanced players to win a point outright or to maneuver their opponents out of position. Even though you may not be quite ready for intermediate and advanced strokes, these are some of the skills to watch for and to work on during your tennis training.

BALL SPIN

There is probably no such thing as a perfectly "flat" drive or serve in tennis. Some degree of spin occurs each time the ball is hit. The flat stroke refers to a ball hit squarely with a relatively level swing as contrasted with the overspin and underspin drives described in the following paragraphs. Because spin plays an important part in the mastery of the auxiliary strokes, understanding it and the effect it has on the flight and bounce of the ball will assist you in varying your stroke production and in preparing for groundstroke and service returns. When you are able to *control* ball spin and can also play the spinning ball after is bounces, you will be well on your way toward achieving a well-rounded game.

Topspin (Forward Spin, Overspin, or Loop)

To achieve topspin, the racket head starts from a position behind and *below* the ball, strikes the back side, and continues up and through the ball to a high finish. The ball spins in the direction of the stroke and, when coupled with the forces of gravity and air resistance, drops swiftly to the ground. As a result of the overspin, the ball travels faster after the bounce than before—it shoots up and out. Because of the sharp drop of the ball during its flight (it seems to dip downward), this shot is used against a net rusher to force him to hit the ball defensively from below the top of the net. The application of topspin to ground-

Fig. 3.1 Ball Spin

strokes provides a greater margin of error since the shot crosses the net higher than the typical flat shot and drops sharply well within the baseline. This permits the hitter to hit the ball harder while still retaining control. Figure 3.1 assumes that the topspin shot (C) is hit harder than either the backspin shot (A) or the flat shot (B). Various topspins are also used when serving and are discussed in a later section.

Backspin (Underspin, Chop, or Slice)

The backspin is the reverse of the topspin. The ball, after being hit, turns away from the direction in which it is moving. To achieve underspin, the racket head starts from a position behind and *above* the ball, strikes the back side, and continues down and through the ball. Underspin causes the ball to rise slightly after contact, thus producing a floating type of flight. When it hits the ground, it loses much of its forward momentum. It may either "hug" the ground or bounce up, depending on the type of underspin (chip, chop, slice). The underspin return is used both offensively and defensively and is especially useful for high backhand returns, low volleys, and short angle approach shots.

Sidespin

Although not as popular, sidespin is used by some players when hitting down-the-line shots or when using an extreme slice on the serve. When hitting a drive, the ball is caused to spin on the vertical axis by drawing the racket strings across the ball toward the body. This causes the ball to spin like a top. The ball, when it bounces, tends to slide in the direction of the spin.

THE ADVANCED SERVES

The serve must be varied to keep your opponent from getting set and grooving his return. Variation may occur by changing speed, spin, or direction. The two most popular advanced serves are the *slice* and the *twist*. When combined with the flat serve, they provide you with all the ammunition you need to go after your opponent.

Slice

The slice is similar to the flat serve. Just a few slight differences in mechanics produce the slice or sliding effect. The service grip described earlier, halfway between the forehand (p. 8) and backhand grips (p. 13), is more flexible and is desirable for advanced serves. The ball is tossed and struck to the right of center, approximately a foot in front of the right shoulder. The racket face is slightly closed and strikes the ball on the upper right section at an angle that will cause it to spin in the direction of the left sideline (fig. 2.8). The follow-through is out, a little to the right of the intended direction of the serve, and the finish is toward the left side of the body. The slice serve is used to draw the receiver off the court or to spin the ball into his body. It eventually becomes the basic delivery for most players.

Twist (Topspin Serve)

The twist, sometimes called the topspin or the American Twist, is difficult to learn and should not be seriously attempted until both the flat and slice services have been mastered. The twist varies from the former serves in that the ball is tossed up to the left and slightly behind the head so that the server must bring his racket well up and over the ball from left to right (fig. 2.8). The diagonal overspin applied to the ball causes it to "kick" or "hop" up to the receiver's backhand. The body bends backward in an arch and together with arm, wrist, and racket snaps up and out at the hit. The follow-through is far to the right, although, after the hit and the initial follow-through, the finish may be on the left side as in the other serves.

THE LOB

When your opponent rushes the net, your play is a drive down the line, a short crosscourt shot or a lob. The lob can keep the net rusher honest and may be a significant factor, as it has on many occasions, in the outcome of the match. In addition, it provides valuable time for the player drawn out of position by an opponent's placement. Don't underestimate the value of the lob. Learn it well and use it.

The lob is started the same way as the groundstrokes, whether on the forehand or backhand side. Grip, stance, and backswing are identical, and the tournament player uses this initial movement to disguise his offensive lob and thus wins many points outright. The difference between the drive and the lob lies in the angle of the racket face as contact is made with the ball and in the finish of the stroke. It may be hit with either topspin or underspin and demands all of the timing and precision of the other strokes, possibly a little more. Because of the higher trajectory of the lob, the racket head starts lower than in the normal drive. The stroke through the ball will vary in accordance with the lobber's intentions.

Two types of lobs are generally distinguished—the offensive and the defensive. The offensive lob is hit either flat or with overspin just over the opponent's reach and is used primarily against a net rusher. In doubles, it is mixed up with crosscourt returns to keep the netman from moving too far and too often from his position. The flat lob is difficult to control and is not used as much as the overspin. Overspin lends an element of control and, at the same time, causes the ball to jump away from the opponent after the bounce. Remember that the offensive lob is most effective when disguised, so don't give away your intentions.

The defensive lob is usually hit with some degree of underspin which causes the ball to slow down and hang in the air. This gives the lobber, who has probably been forced out of position, time to get back to a more favorable court position. When lobbing defensively, remember the length of the court from baseline to baseline and hit the ball to go the distance.

Learn to lob offensively and defensively with both forehand and backhand. A beginner frequently attempts to drive the ball past his opponent, even when he is hopelessly out of position. This aversion to the lob and to other dink shots usually gives the opponent the edge at the net. With experience, players soon realize the importance of the lob and use it more often.

THE OVERHEAD OR SMASH

The answer to the lob is the overhead or smash. It is one of the most vital shots in tennis. Lack of a good overhead will defeat a good net attack while ability to smash will provide the weapon to finish off many rallies. The overhead stroke, in many ways, is similar to the serve. The main difference is that the ball is tossed up by the opponent—not the smasher—and the player must move to get into position to hit the ball. There are two basic overhead shots, the smash at the net and the smash from the baseline where the ball is taken after the bounce. Both are important, and time must be taken to learn them well.

The grip is basically the same as that used for the serve with the fingers well spread for control. The smash is hit fairly flat, especially when close to the net. Body position and action is the same as for the serve once the player has reached the position from which he will execute the shot. To reach the desired position, turn your side to the net and *slide back* under the lob, or if the lob is very deep, you may have to turn and *run back*. But in each case, the player should reach a position *behind* the desired point of contact in which the body is turned sideways with the feet spread and the weight on the back foot. Pointing at the ball with your left hand helps in keeping your eye on the ball (fig. 3.2) and in getting you into the desired position. The racket is drawn almost straight back and up with a definite pause behind the shoulder with the elbow high and racket head hanging down. The ball is hit about one foot in front of the head and as high as possible with a flat racket face. Direction is controlled by the use of arm and wrist, the wrist snapping forward and downward at the moment of impact. The angle of the racket varies according to the distance

| Ready | Turn | Sight | Hit | Finish |

Fig. 3.2   The Overhead Smash

from the net—sharper when close, less as the player moves back. The racket follows through in the direction of the shot.

A deep lob to be returned after the ball has bounced may be played as a smash or as a groundstroke. The hitter must learn to judge the bounce of the ball which will vary because of the spin imparted to it by the opponent. The smasher must move back fast enough to be prepared to meet the ball in front of the body. In order to smash, the rebound must be high enough to be hit as an overhead. When the smasher is deep in his own court, the trajectory of the smash is often tempered by the use of spin, usually slice, and the shot is placed, not hit for a winner. If you have a good serve, you can have a good overhead.

DROPSHOTS AND DROP VOLLEYS

Dropshots and drop volleys are the whipped cream of a player's game and are very definite complements to the all-around game.

The *dropshot* is used to draw a baseline player in to the net, to move a slow player who has been caught deep in his own backcourt, or to wear down an opponent by drawing him in and then forcing him back with a subsequent lob. It is a very delicate shot and is usually attempted when the stroker is in front of his own baseline. The closer you are to the net, the more effective the shot is likely to be.

The dropshot is executed after the ball has bounced and may be hit with varying degrees of backspin. The backswing is similar to that of the normal groundstroke. As the ball is contacted, the wrist turns under and imparts underspin to the ball, slowing down its forward motion. The follow-through is downward and relatively short. The ball is hit to the side and in front of the body with an open racket face.

It is necessary to drop the ball over and as close to the net as possible. If it is too deep, the opponent will be in position to make a forcing shot and may even win the point outright on his first stroke.

The *drop volley* depends on a very small amount of wrist action at the instant the ball is hit. The racket face is slightly open at impact, the face of the racket moving under the ball so that at the finish, it is almost completely open. Relaxing the wrist at impact ("giving" with the ball) causes the ball to lose some of its speed and has somewhat the same effect as throwing a ball against a hanging drape.

Drop volleys are used only when the player is at the net. Like the drop shot, it must be dropped just over the net, and it will backfire on the volleyer if the opponent can reach the ball. Angle the ball away from your opponent whenever possible. A good rule to follow is not to use the drop volley if the ball can be put away with a deeper volley.

HALF-VOLLEY

The half-volley is neither a volley nor a groundstroke but a defensive shot hit on the rise immediately after the bounce. It has often been compared to the drop-kick in football. There will be many occasions when you will be trapped as you move to the net and do not have time to get into position for a forcing volley or cannot volley at all. You have already covered several yards of court space, consequently you must adjust your stroke by keeping both backswing and follow-through to a minimum. Actually, you place your racket behind the ball so the racket meets the ball instead of the racket moving forward to meet the ball. The speed of the ball as it rebounds from the court surface provides the power for the return. The point of impact is in front of the player.

The shot is controlled by the angle of the racket face, and this increases in importance as you move closer to the net. The face is opened as you approach the net to raise the ball. However, when you half-volley from the backcourt, the face is closed to prevent the ball from rising too high on the return. With practice, you will learn to adjust your racket to attain the proper trajectory.

FOOTWORK AND TIMING

Good footwork and timing are the trademarks of the finished player. How often have you watched an athletic contest and thought to yourself, "My, how easy they make it look!" This ease of execution comes only after hours of hard work, work on the basic strokes and work on the means of getting into the best position to execute them with as near perfect weight control and balance as possible. And timing, which some people are fortunate to be born with, can be learned so well that it becomes automatic. You can incorporate these attributes into your game by practicing the footwork suggestions made in chapter 2, by using the practice drills described in the next chapter, and by applying the suggestions on tactics found in chapter 5. Eventually, you, too, will make it look easy.

Progress can be speeded up

4

There are many ways to speed your progress, only a few of which are presented here. Of course, one of the best ways is to play frequently against all kinds of opponents. However, playing tennis does not provide enough practice on your specific weaknesses; thus, some form of concentrated practice on specific aspects of performance will probably be beneficial in improving your game.

GENERAL CONDITIONING AND WARM-UP

Tennis is a strenuous game when played competitively, and it requires a certain amount of physical conditioning. Conditioning includes proper diet, adequate rest periods, and a good mental attitude as well as exercises designed to develop stamina, agility, flexibility, strength, neuromuscular coordination, and speed.

Exercises, which approximate the demands of actual competition in which vigorous effort is interspersed with brief opportunities for rest (that is, between points and while changing courts), meet the criterion of specificity. This criterion, which is an important principle in improving performance, demands that the exercises utilized in a conditioning program be specifically related to and impose stresses similar to those of the activity for which the conditioning is being done. Running is one of the best conditioners for tennis, and a running schedule based on wind sprints (a run-jog-sprint series) will develop cardio-respiratory endurance as well as speed and leg strength. Forward and backward running, including sudden starts and stops, quick changes in direction, skipping and sliding sideways, running up and down stairs, and running in place at varied tempos are all good. Use these to warm up at the beginning of your practice period and, to increase strength and endurance, repeat them at the termination of practice when you are tired. Work done when tired produces an overload which is essential in increasing strength and endurance. If you stop practice at the first sign of fatigue you may have reached a minor psychological barrier, but you are still far from the physiological limits of your performance. Since no overload will have occurred, no real change in condition will result.

When playing doubles, which combination of letters represents the best positions for both players? A-B? C-D? E-F? Why?
What shots might be used to attack a team in position A-B? C-D? E-F?

Rope skipping is another popular warm-up and coordination exercise which you may use to supplement the running exercises.

Lunging forward, sideward, and diagonally forward to both the forehand and backhand sides, and using the crossover step will increase your ability to play balls when you are slightly out of position. Combine the lunges with running in place, and return to the running position immediately after each lunge.

The following are also recommended.

1. Squeeze a tennis or sponge ball to develop the strength of the muscles used in gripping the racket.

2. Do pushups and sit-ups to develop arm, shoulder girdle, and abdominal strength.

3. Practice stroking with the cover on the racket (include the press as strength increases).

Remember, these exercises do not take the place of hitting tennis balls, but they should not be neglected. Use discrimination in the amount of time you spend on each, but include some type of specific exercise in your schedule. As you become a more finished player, you will need to increase the work load in order to further improve strength, stamina, reaction time, and overall coordination.

PRACTICE DRILLS WITH RACKET AND BALL

This section provides exercises and drills to help you master tennis skills. Some are for beginners, others for intermediate players, and still others are quite advanced. Most of the drills include suggestions for making the practice situation progressively more difficult. Some of these you can practice alone, some with a partner, and others with members of your group. Always keep the following concept in mind—practice makes perfect when the practice is *purposeful*, is done in *good form*, and achieves the desired results. Shorter periods of time during which real practice occurs will be much more effective than longer periods of time spent in half-hearted effort. Just as overloading is an important principle in developing strength and endurance, so is overlearning an important principle in developing skills. *Thousands* of balls must be hit *correctly* before the skills will become automatic. Concentrate! Work hard! Soon, you will find your game developing into the type you had hoped for.

Without a Partner

Backboard Rally   From distances of 5, 25, and 39 feet, stroke a ball against the backboard using the basic groundstrokes. Add the net line to the backboard and resume practice. Play the ball on any bounce at first, concentrating on form and hitting it correctly. Later, when correct stroking form is habitual, play the ball on one bounce, hustle into position, and concentrate on footwork.

Serving Practice   When serving form has become consistent and correct, place a hula hoop or a tennis ball can on one of the desirable aim points (identified in the self-evaluation question p. 45) and practice hitting your serve to a specified aim point. Move the target to several of the desirable aim points and practice in both service courts. Be sure to maintain correct form while practicing. Do not sacrifice speed and spin in order to gain accuracy.

Volley Practice   Stand approximately ten feet from the backboard, and practice volleying a ball against it. Spend the last five minutes of each practice session volleying with the cover on the racket.

Stroke Developer Practice   If you have a stroke developer (ball suspended on elastic shock cord fig. 4.1), use it whenever you can to groove your groundstrokes, serve, and volley. Strive for perfection.

Tethered (Rebound) Ball   Stroke the tethered ball (fig. 4.1) across the net and keep it in play either on the forehand or backhand side at first, then alternating forehand and backhand strokes.

Fig. 4.1   Stroke Developer and Tethered Ball

With a Partner

When you have a partner to work with, your practice drills can be more fun, especially if you inject the element of competition. At the same time, you will be able to help one another by making corrections and suggestions.

Partner Drop and Hit   From the side-to-net position, stroke balls, dropped by your partner, across the net and deep into the opposite court. You and your partner should be standing behind one baseline about three feet away from each other, and your partner should *drop* the ball at the perfect point of impact for your swing. Select target areas for placement practice. When hitting to backcourt targets, the ball should clear the net by three or four feet.

Toss and Hit Across the Net   This drill is similar to drop and hit drill except that you start in the ready position and the ball is tossed to you instead of dropped. Vary the practice by having your partner toss long and short balls, some right at you, others away from you.

Rally Practice   Using the service court lines as boundaries, keep the ball in play by hitting the ball back and forth across the net. Start each rally with a self-drop and hit. Later, move behind the baselines, and use the regulation court. Play the ball on any bounce at first—concentrate on form and on hitting it correctly. Later, when correct stroking form is habitual, play the ball on one bounce, hustle into position, and concentrate on footwork.

Deep Court Game   Draw lines approximately nine feet inside of and parallel to both baselines. Play a set, using a baseline game (Rushing the net is against the rules of this game!), counting every ball falling short of the nine-foot line as an out ball. Later, follow "short" balls in toward the net, and attempt to volley.

Placement Drill   Beginning with a self-drop and hit, stroke the ball across the net attempting to hit it to your partner's forehand. Keep the rally going, attempting to hit every ball to his forehand. Later, practice placing all your shots to his backhand. Both players should return to the center of the baseline after each hit. Be sure to reverse roles so that your partner can practice his placements, too! As your skill increases, add difficulty by combining the deep court game with placement practice. With three players, A hitting against B and C, player A hits crosscourt shots while players B and C hit down-the-line shots. Players rotate clockwise at specified intervals.

Serve and Return of Serve   Serve to both right and left service courts to your partner who will return the serve. Alternate staying back and advancing to the net after each serve. The receiver attempts to return balls deep when you stay back and attempts to play the return short and low when you rush the net. Do not attempt to volley the return at first—concentrate on the serve and the return. You may volley and play out the point later.

Volley Practice   From a good volleying position at the net, volley balls that have been stroked to you from the baseline. At first, have your practice partner hit only to your forehand side, then only to your backhand. Then be prepared to volley shots hit in any direction—to your forehand or backhand, right at you, high or low. Rotate roles so your partner can practice the volley too. When volleying, concentrate on keeping both the backswing and forward swing as short as possible.

With three players, player A volleying from a *net* position against players

In hitting a volley, do you:

1. Keep sight of your racket during the backswing?
2. Punch the ball, using a minimum stroke?
3. Keep your wrist firm on impact?
4. Meet the ball **well out in front** of you?
5. Keep your racket head above your wrist?
6. Bend your knees for low balls?

B and C stationed behind the baseline, player A aims each volley alternately to the deep corners. Since there are two players behind the baseline, player A can volley aggressively, while players B and C try to get every volley after one bounce, and return shots designed to make player A stretch and scramble. Rotate to all three positions.

With two players standing near their respective service lines on opposite sides of the net, volley against your partner. Try to keep the ball in play at first, and then volley low to make him hit up to you. Finally try to volley past each other.

Lob and Smash Practice   One or two players start in a good net position and smash against two players lobbing from behind the baseline. Exchange positions at intervals. While the lobbers should concentrate on retrieving every smash, the smashers should hustle into good position under each lob and work on meeting the ball squarely, as high as possible, and out in front.

There are many other fine practice drills which might be used. In addition, you can devise practice situations to suit your own needs. Practice situations should be game-like, should demand correct performance of skills, and should place increasing stress on the player. Whatever the situation, remember that the way you perform the skills while practicing is what counts. Fundamentals build sound foundations, so don't count on luck, depend on skill!

THE GRADUATED LENGTH METHOD

A very popular and successful method of learning the basic tennis skills is the one known as the GLM or "graduated length method." It is similar to that used by many ski instructors in which students start with short skis and gradually progress to the full-length ones. In most cases, students are able to experience early success which in turn motivates them and keeps them from experiencing frustration. For the student having difficulty in learning to control the full-sized racket, the GLM may be the answer.

The GLM is based on the theory that an individual is able to control and to adjust more quickly to activity in the area immediately in front of and close to the body. As the distance between the body and the end of the lever increases, some learners experience more difficulty in controlling and adjusting their movements. It is important to understand that the movements of the hand, arm, feet, and the rest of the body utilized in stroking are similar, regardless of whether the student is holding or simulating holding a racket. Holding the racket at the face, the throat, the shaft, or just above the leather changes the length of the lever. Shortening the lever reduces the tension on the wrist and makes for better control. Because of this, the stroking pattern is more easily and quickly learned. Graduation to the full grip and stroke progresses smoothly.

The following presentation is a condensed version of the GLM, not an in-depth analysis. For the student experiencing difficulty in controlling the full-size racket in the beginning, this could provide the means of making a satisfactory adjustment. For the advanced player having difficulty with stroke production, "going back to basics" may be a means of overcoming this problem. Two directions may be taken in the "simplified approach." GLM progressions may take place by starting with the hand, moving to the paddle, then the short racket and finally, the full-size racket. Another way to utilize a GLM progression is to start with the hand, then hold the full-size racket at the face, then at the throat, at the shaft, and finally at the regular grip. Because most students have a full-size racket, the latter procedure will be described here.

The Groundstrokes

The analysis of the stroking pattern for the forehand and backhand drives is the same as that described earlier in the book (chap. 2), except that the racket is not used until the desired stroke pattern is mastered using only the hand (fig. 4.2). Following is a suggested progression.

Fig. 4.2   GLM—Using the Hand

1. Ball bounce drills—bouncing the ball down to the court, then bouncing the ball upward.
2. Stroking drills from a self-drop and from the side-to-net (stroking) position—the player drops the ball straight down, steps forward, and strokes the ball. Stroking practice can be against a fence, a backboard, or with a partner at a distance of from 15 to 20 feet.
3. Stroking drills from the ready position again using a self-drop. Appropriate cue words would be turn, step, swing.

4. With a partner tossing the ball to the hitter waiting in the ready position, the hitter strokes the ball back to the tosser. During this period, the ball is stroked only a short distance (15 to 20 feet).

The steps listed above are practiced using the palm of the hand and extended fingers to contact the ball. Emphasis is placed on maintaining a firm wrist. When these steps are mastered, the player begins with the racket, holding the racket by placing the spread fingers on the strings (fig. 4.3). The progression is then repeated.

From the strings, the hand is moved to the throat of the racket, and the progression is repeated. Ball toss practice should include alternating tosses to the forehand and the backhand. As the hand moves down the shaft of the racket, the distance between partners is increased. At the same time, the backswing and thrust through the ball are lengthened. When the grip reaches the point where the hand is touching the leather of the grip, the students move to the court and balls are hit across the net. At first, balls are hit from halfway between the service line and baseline, then from behind the baseline. Rallying is added to the progression.

Fig. 4.3 GLM—Holding the Throat

The groundstroke progression is completed when the player has mastered the rally using the regular grip on the racket. The length of time spent on each phase of the GLM must not be rushed. The student must allow time to master each phase before moving on to the next. Patience is the key to successful learning. Above all, practice, practice, practice.

The Serve

Like the groundstroke progression, the serve may be learned with a paddle and short racket, or with the normal tennis racket. Again, this presentation will disregard the paddle and short racket. The basic serving motion is very much like that of an overhand throw, so practice begins throwing balls overhand to a partner or against a wall. The left foot is placed at a 45° angle to the baseline and is kept in place during the throw. Emphasis is placed on a flexible wrist-elbow action. The throw is an overhand motion and the wrist is rotated so that the back of the hand moves toward the face at the finish.

The ball toss, as described earlier (p. 17), is practiced next. Following is a suggested GLM progression.

1. First, the coordination of the two arms is begun. The left hand executes the ball toss while the right hand, starting with the elbow high and the hand behind the right ear, practices a "reach and catch" pattern. After the catch, the right hand and arm should move through the complete pattern of fol-low-through and finish.

2. Next, starting in the same position, the right arm extends through the swing and the right palm and extended fingers contact the ball which is hit to the wall or to a partner.

3. While holding the racket at the throat, start with the right elbow shoulder high and the racket head behind the player's head. The ball is tossed up by the left hand, and the player reaches up (extends) the right arm and hits through the ball. Practice against a wall or fence.

4. Next, standing behind the service line and holding the racket at the shaft, the player serves over the net and into the appropriate service court by using the half-swing serving motion described above.

5. Standing behind the baseline and holding the racket at the regular grip, the player practices serving over the net into the service court still using the half-swing serve.

6. Standing behind the baseline, the player practices the full-swing serve, as analyzed in chapter 2, by using the regular grip on the racket.

The Volley

The GLM progression for volleying is similar to that followed for the ground-strokes and the serve. In this progression, one partner tosses a ball underhand (a "friendly" toss) directly to the appropriate target. By tossing correctly, the tosser forces the learner to use the crossover step, to shift the weight forward, and to execute the task with proper mechanics.

1. The volleyer steps forward with the left foot, and with the right hand catches a ball tossed in front of his right shoulder by a partner who is about 15 feet away. Emphasis is placed on keeping the elbow down and on inter-cepting the ball as soon as possible.

2. Next, the "volleyer" starts in a ready position, then turns, steps, and reaches forward to catch the toss.

3. Starting from a ready position, the volleyer then "volleys" the ball with the extended fingers back to the tosser.

4. Following hand practice, the fingers are placed behind the strings of the racket and the volleyer volleys the ball back to the tosser so the tosser can catch it on the fly. For backhand volley practice, place the thumb behind

the strings. Continue to emphasize stepping toward the ball, meeting it well out in front.

5. Repeat the previous step holding the racket at the throat. Move the grip down the shaft and repeat again. As the grip moves down the shaft, the distance between partners is increased, but the volleyer must volley gently enough so that the tosser can catch the volley. Concentrate on keeping both the backswing and forward swing as short as possible. At first, toss only to the forehand, then, only to the backhand, and then, alternate tosses to the forehand and backhand.

6. From a volleying position at the net, the volleyer, using the regular grip on the racket, volleys balls tossed to him by his partner. Vary tosses to the forehand and backhand. Toss some balls right at the volleyer (use a backhand volley to protect yourself). Toss at different levels, some high, some low. Watch the ball and change the angle of the racket face (closed for high balls, open for low ones).

7. From a volleying position at the net, volley balls that have been stroked to you from the baseline. Volley deep to both corners.

8. With one player at the net and one in the backcourt, add rallying to the progression.

In utilizing any of the suggested GLM progressions, patience cannot be overly stressed. It takes time to master each phase of the progression before going on to the next. As the hand moves down the shaft of the racket, it becomes apparent that the stroke through the ball must be made with more authority. The stroke becomes longer, and the weight shift more pronounced. The transition from the hand to the full racket takes place naturally—and "painlessly."

Patterns of play

5

Specific rules of strategy for every possible situation cannot be established. There are, however, general principles that every player can apply to his own game. Skill in stroking is not the only requirement for a winning game. Players must utilize brain power and must possess a will to win. Once you realize that the thinking player has an advantage, you will have taken a very large step forward in improving your performance. That tennis is a game requiring skill cannot be denied, but inability to use the available skill most effectively is often the cause of a losing game. Following are some of the more important principles which can be applied to your game.

1.   **Play through your strengths to your opponent's weaknesses.** Weaknesses may be inherent stroke weaknesses, or they may be created by moving your opponent out of position. A common stroke weakness of many players is the backhand, but individual players may have other weaknesses as well. Learn to recognize these and strive to exploit them. The warm-up period just prior to a match provides an excellent beginning for these observations, but remember to keep alert throughout the match. If your opponent likes hard drives, hit soft-angled balls with a variety of spin; if he has a good net game, keep him in the backcourt with passing shots and lobs; if he does not like to play net, force him up with dropshots, and then give him a difficult volley to handle. Be careful about playing his weakness too often, since obviously, he will try to protect it. Hit an occasional shot to his forehand, thus making the next shot to his back-hand more difficult for him to handle. A player may improve his weakness dur-ing match play because his opponent continually plays to it, thus giving him the practice he evidently needs. Save the shot to his weakness until you really need a point, when you're behind 15-40 or when you finally get the advantage in a long deuce game. Remember, too, that his strongest stroke may not be his steadiest.

Remember, also, that you must plan your strategy around the shots which you can execute successfully. If you do not have a good net game, it is pure folly to charge the net at every opportunity just because you think it is the way to beat a particular opponent. Instead, stay in the backcourt and play the shots you can hit effectively. *Plan your strategy around your strengths.*

2.   **Anticipate.** This is one of the best general rules although admittedly quite difficult to use effectively. It is possible, however, so start developing this quality *right now! Where you hit the ball* governs the possibilities your opponent has in making his return. In addition, you must *analyze your opponent's pattern of play.* Does he usually hit a deep forehand down the line or crosscourt? Where does he usually return a backhand? Many players have great difficulty hitting a backhand down the line. (They're really just lazy and need to move their feet into the proper position!) If your opponent falls into this category, you can hit a deep shot to his backhand, advance to the net, and be waiting to volley away his customary crosscourt return. Anticipation requires that you divert some of your attention away from the ball in order to *watch* your opponent. Notice *how he hits* the ball, for his methods of stroke production will frequently give away his intent. For example, if he contacts the ball late, it will probably go down the line, and if he hits it early, most likely it will go crosscourt. If his backswing is high, he will probably impart backspin to the ball, and if the backswing is low, the ball will usually carry topspin. Note the location of his ball toss when he serves (also the angle of his racket face), and you may be able to profit from your keen observation. Anticipation enables you to cover more court, get more balls back, get yourself in better position to hit the ball, and play a better game more easily. It is most discouraging to an opponent who thinks he has a ball put away, to see you move easily a few steps and return it effectively, just because you know all along where he was going to hit and got a head start in that direction.

3.   **Keep your opponent moving.** Make him run from one side to the other, up and then back, from one short angle to a long, deep angle. Never let him get set. Many players may be able to run from side to side quite well, but there are few people who can run up and back and still make effective returns. There is some danger in hitting short balls, but the effective combination of dropshots followed by lobs is a very difficult one to beat. And when you finally do maneuver him out of position, don't become overanxious or excited trying to blast a winner into the opening. (You will probably hit it over the fence!) Just watch the ball, get into a good stroking position, and concentrate on hitting the shot well.

4.   **Change the pace.** Keep your opponent off-balance and guessing all the time. Vary the speed, the spin, and the placement of your shots. Hit one ball hard and deep, the next one deep but softer, the third one angled short with topspin, and the fourth one deep with backspin.

5.   **Remember that more points are "lost" on errors than "won" on placements.** Concentrate on steadiness, accuracy, and consistency. Let your opponent make the errors. Do not try to make your shots too good. Give yourself a margin of safety. When playing from the backcourt, keep your shots *deep* with medium height and medium speed. If your opponent has successfully applied some of the principles previously described and has moved you out of position, your best choice of return is probably a long crosscourt drive rather than a drive down the

If you must return the ball from point X, would you aim your shot to point Y or Z? Why?

line. The net is lower in the center than at the sidelines, and the court is longer, by approximately six feet, from one corner to the other than down the line. Thus, your margin of error is greater on the crosscourt, and, since this shot travels the longer distance, it also gives you more time to recover your position.

6. **Bisect the angle of your opponent's possible returns.** This is a basic theory of position play which says that as soon as you hit the ball, you *immediately* place yourself in the best possible position to defend your court. *DON'T WAIT* to see whether your shot will be in; if you do, you won't be ready for the next shot. *AND DON'T STAND THERE ADMIRING* your shot, for while you're doing that, your opponent may be hitting it back past you. The ready position you know about already. The best court position is usually in the *middle* of the return *angle* available to your opponent, not necessarily in the middle of the court. This angle will change with every shot you hit, thus the direction of your shot is an important determining factor. The long crosscourt drive advocated above puts you at least two steps closer to bisecting the angle than would a down-the-line shot.

7. **Do not change a winning game—always change a losing game.** If the strategy you decide upon is working well and you are winning, keep it up. Do not relax, let up, or start practicing some new, fancy shot. Your opponent may suddenly catch fire, and you probably will not be able to return to your previous level of play. However, if your opponent begins to utilize some effective strategy of his own, then you must change your tactics. If you are losing, by all means, try something else. You have nothing further to lose by trying other tactics, and you might find the answer to your opponent's game. Keep looking for his weaknesses, keep your eyes on the ball, concentrate on getting every ball back, and perhaps the tide of the match will turn in your favor.

In addition to these general principles, there are certain situations in which every player will find himself during the course of a match. The following are a few suggestions which may be helpful when a player finds himself in that particular situation.

SERVICE

Stance

In singles, it is generally best to stand near the center mark to serve, although some players prefer to stand about three feet to the left of the center mark when serving to the left court, thus making it easier to serve to the receiver's back-

Fig. 5.1   Doubles Serving Position

hand. Note that when the server stands near the center mark, immediately after the serve, he is almost in the position from which he can best defend his own court against the return of serve. If the serve is placed near the center line, the server has automatically "bisected the angle" (principle 6 above). Serving consistently from the same position will increase accuracy.

In doubles, the server's stance should be approximately in the center of the half of the court which the server must cover immediately after the serve. The server's partner is customarily stationed in a good net position, about six to eight feet from the net, on the other half of the court, and as close to the center line as he can be without jeopardizing the defense of his alley against a down-the-line service return. The server's partner takes this position on the assumption that his partner will also come to a net position, preferably behind his serve, but if not then, as soon as possible thereafter (fig. 5.1). Basic positioning for doubles teams demands that partners play side by side in a parallel relationship to each other. The up and back formation is ineffective in covering the court since it leaves openings along both sidelines and also diagonally through the middle.

Placement

Usually, the serve should be deep to either corner of the service court and should force your opponent to return the ball with his weakest stroke, in most cases his backhand. However, occasional serves to his strong side will prevent him from covering up his weakness and will keep him from getting set and grooving his return. Some serves should be delivered directly at him, and the pace and spin of the serves should be varied. The most common mistake in service strategy is a fireball first service (along with a prayer to help it go in!), and then, if the first serve misses, a slow dinky second serve (which any self-respecting receiver would hit away for a winner). Players would do better to develop a reliable first serve with medium pace and spin and a second serve only slightly slower and with slightly more spin than the first ball. In doubles, the slower, spinning, and higher bouncing twist or topspin serve is usually advocated, thereby giving the server more time to advance to the net immediately after the serve. The flat serve hit with great speed is not too effective as a means of getting to the net because the return is usually past the server before he can get more than two or three steps into the court.

RETURN OF SERVE

This is one of the most important aspects of tennis. The position for receiving the serve will, of course, depend upon the type of serve your opponent is using. In singles, if it is a fast or high bouncing serve, it is best to stand back of the baseline and just inside the imaginary continuation of the singles sideline. For slower or lower bouncing balls, one or two steps forward is a more aggressive position. The return of service should employ as many of the suggested principles as possible, but in many cases, particularly if your opponent has a good first serve, it is better to concentrate simply on getting the ball back. If your opponent has a very fast serve, you will probably not have time to stroke the ball with a full-swing groundstroke. Instead, attempt to block the ball back, merely letting the ball rebound from your racket, and concentrate on controlling the direction of your return. The return should be as deep as possible (unless the server is rushing the net) and away from the server, preferably to his weak side. If your opponent has a weak second serve, *step in* and take the advantage away from him with an aggressive and forcing return. Don't try for an outright winner unless you have an easy return. Hit as forcefully as you can without error. Use less force if you have to, but *keep the ball in play*.

In doubles, the receiver stands near the baseline and the singles sideline, and his partner stands in the middle of the other half of the court just inside the service line (fig. 5.2). If your opponent serves and immediately rushes the net, you should try to return the serve crosscourt to the server's feet, somewhere near the service line. This type of return will force the onrushing server to make a low and rather difficult volley or half-volley. If you are successful in returning crosscourt, both you and your partner move up into a good net position, but if the return is weak or to the serving team's netman, the receiver's

Fig. 5.2   Doubles Receiving Position

partner retreats to the baseline. His starting position is intermediary between offense and defense, and he moves one way or the other depending upon the receiver's return. If the server's partner anticipates your customary crosscourt return and begins to poach effectively, you might try driving a return down the line behind the crossing netman or lobbing the return over the netman's head. These are the three basic choices that the receiver has when returning a serve, and skillful variation of the pattern can be a most effective strategy. If your skills are not yet quite up to this net rushing style of play, both partners of the receiving team should play back behind the baseline in order to maintain parallel positioning.

PLAYING IN THE BACKCOURT

Against Another Baseline Player

In singles, this may happen often: The two opponents stay near the baseline and try to "outsteady" each other, each player making innumerable trips from one sideline to the other and each point finally being decided after the ball has made thirty or forty trips from one end of the court to the other. If patience and stamina are factors in your favor, this strategy may work for you. However, it is usually much more interesting to apply some of the principles mentioned previously. Try to pull your opponent up to the net with a dropshot, and then chase him to the baseline after a lob. Keep your own shots deep, and, if your opponent hits a short shot to you, utilize this opportunity to attack by moving in to hit it on the rise.

Against a Net Rusher

This situation occurs often in doubles when one team is on the offense in command of the net and the other team is forced into defensive play at the baseline. There are only three choices for the baseline players. First, they can lob over the heads of the net players and thereby dislodge them from the net. The primary danger of this choice is lobbing too low or too short, thus giving the net players an opportunity to win the point with a smash. The second choice is to hit a passing shot for an outright winner. When trying this down either sideline, there is danger of trying to make the shot too good and hitting slightly long or wide or into the net. One of the best targets for a passing shot is the center of the court. The net is lowest in the center giving you a greater margin of safety, and your opponents may also become confused about who should cover center balls. (The player whose forehand is in the center generally covers.) The third choice is to hit a relatively soft and low shot so that the net players will be forced to volley up. Many strategists insist that the basic idea behind all shots in doubles is to force your opponents to volley up, thus enabling you to win the point by hitting down past their feet.

In singles, the choices are the same. A good lob should dislodge your opponent from the net position and should prevent him from crowding the net in the future, thus making your low shots more effective. Passing shots are probably used more often in singles than in doubles because the net player has more court to cover in singles, so the passing shots have more possibility for success. Remember that the net player will try to anticipate your return, so keep him guessing. If you hit a shot which he can reach, do a little anticipating yourself, and try to get a head start in the probable direction of this volley. If you are a good guesser, you may be able to turn what should have been a winning volley for him into a winning passing shot for you.

Whenever you play against a successful net rusher, do all you can to keep him in the backcourt away from the net. Make his advance to the net as hazardous as possible by keeping the ball deep to his weakness. If he does get an opportunity to come in, try to hit your next shot to his feet, thus forcing him to make a difficult volley. If you do force him to make this low volley, anticipate a weak and short return, and move in a couple of steps so that you will be in good position to hit a potential winner.

PLAYING AT THE NET

Against a Baseline Player

If you are hitting from *inside your own baseline*, you have a good opportunity to advance to the net. Try to hit your approach shot deep, thus forcing your opponent to hit from *behind his baseline* and preferably with his weakness. The approach shot should put your opponent on the defensive and should permit you to obtain a suitable position for protecting your own court, thus down the line is usually a better choice than crosscourt. The approach shot itself is not intended to be a winner, therefore, it is neither necessary nor advisable to hit with extreme power. Usually a medium-paced, well-placed shot is most desirable since the medium speed provides the time needed by the net rusher to move from the backcourt to the forecourt, and appropriate placement puts the opponent on the defensive.

Get as far into the forecourt as possible to make your first volley, but wherever you are in the court, *stop moving forward* and *get set before you make the shot*. It is quite possible that you may not be in good enough position to make your first volley a winner. If not, try to volley the ball deep and as far away from your opponent as possible, with the hope that you will be able to improve your position for the next volley. If you have made a good approach shot, forcing your opponent to make a weak return, and if you have achieved good position, try to make your first volley crisp and decisive so that it will be a winner. If your opponent can get to your volley, be sure that you bisect the angle of possible return. There is some danger in hitting angled volleys unless they are outright winners because, if your opponent gets to the shot, he has an extremely wide angle into which he can hit. Probably, the best advice is to volley deep to his backcourt until you can force him to hit such a weak return that you can easily volley it on the angle for a put away.

Control of the net is the most important factor in strategy for winning doubles. The two net players must cooperate in dividing the area of possible return. Usually, angled volleys will be useful both as outright winners and as shots designed to maneuver the defending team out of position. Net players

Which of the numbered targets are the most desirable aim points for your first service in singles? Why? In doubles? Why?

should always be aware of the choices available to baseline players and should learn to anticipate passing shots and lobs. When the baseline team succeeds in lobbing over the heads of the net team, both players should retreat to the back-court in order to maintain their parallel formation.

Against Another Net Player

In a singles match, it is relatively rare to find both players at the net simultane-ously. Each player may utilize net play as a basic part of his strategy, but the point usually goes to the player who gets to the net first. Thus, the first serve is quite important since it is often strong enough to provide the server with the opportunity to advance to the net and control the play. It is foolish to rush the net if your opponent is already there, unless you have given him a difficult low volley to handle and therefore anticipate a weak return or a drop volley.

In doubles, the four players are commonly found volleying away at the net. The key to success in this situation is to keep your opponents back toward the service line, forcing them to play defensively while you and your partner play up closer to the net to volley away their rising balls for winners.

To summarize, a winning game requires the following ingredients: first, skill and control of a variety of strokes; second, the utilization of brain power and knowledge of various patterns of play; and third, the will to win. Regardless of your level of skill, strategy and spirit can be important factors in the effec-tiveness of your performance. Even beginners can apply the principles. While some players may prefer to out-hit their opponents, there's a special joy in outwitting opponents!

Rules of the game

6

The International Lawn Tennis Federation establishes rules, considers changes in and interpretations of the existing rules, determines the conditions under which international competition, such as Davis Cup and Federation Cup matches, takes place, and generally supervises the conduct of tennis throughout the world. The United States Tennis Association (formerly the United States Lawn Tennis Association) is a member of the ILTF and thus conducts tennis programs in the United States in a manner consistent with ILTF rules and policies.

While national and international competition is usually conducted in a highly technical manner (*13 officials*, including the umpire, a foot fault judge, and assorted linejudges are used to officiate one singles match between 2 players), the vast majority of tennis competition is conducted without any officials at all. Thus, it is extremely important for each player to assume his obligation to know and follow both the letter and the spirit of the rules. Actually, the official rules have remained unusually stable since the advent of so-called modern tennis in 1877. However, with the growth of professional tennis competition and the development of open tennis, rule changes have been proposed and tried on an experimental basis, but so far, none of the proposed changes have been adopted.

Rules are presented here in an informal manner and some illustrative examples are presented with an attempt to distinguish between the requirements of the rules and the traditions of long-established custom. Numbers in parentheses refer to the official USTA rule number.

The Court and Equipment   Specifications pertaining to the court, its permanent fixtures and equipment are contained in rules 1, 2, and 3 (chap. 1). The exact dimensions of the court are probably not too important to the beginner (or to the tournament player either). However, the *names of the lines* are another matter and should become a part of every player's vocabulary. This knowledge is basic to an understanding of subsequent rules and to any discussion of strategy (fig. 1.1).

SINGLES

The Players and the Toss

In singles, the two players stand on opposite sides of the net. If you are the player who puts the ball into play, you are called the server and your opponent, the receiver. You serve for an entire game, and, at the end of the game, you become the receiver and your opponent becomes the server. You and your opponent alternate serving a game and receiving a game throughout the match (4 and 14).

According to rule (5), contestants decide which one shall serve first and from which side of the net "by toss." The rule does not specify how this toss shall be made. Sometimes a coin is tossed, but, much more frequently, one player places the head of his racket on the ground and spins it like a top. Traditionally, before the spinning racket falls to the ground, the other player calls "rough" or "smooth." These terms refer to the manner in which the trimming strings are wound around the long strings of the racket, so that one face is the rough side and the other face the smooth side. Today most rackets do not have trimming strings and some other means of identifying the two sides of the racket is used, for example, "TAD or Davis," "right side up or upside down," "M or W," "label or no label."

The player winning the toss may choose or require his opponent to choose from among the following: (1) to serve or to receive, and (2) to begin play on the north side or the south side of the court. The player not making the original choice has the choice of the remaining options. Note that if one player chooses the north side, his opponent is *not* automatically required to serve. Instead, the opponent has the remaining choice—to serve or to receive.

Usually, the player who wins the toss elects to serve first. Since many players consider the serve to be the most important offensive weapon, serving first provides not only a mechanical but also a psychological advantage. Occasionally, however, a player may feel that it is to his advantage to receive in the first game, and he will choose accordingly. The opponent, then, must serve the first game, and, in addition has the choice of side. A beginner may feel that his return of serve is stronger than his serve, and, especially if the opponent's serve is rather weak, it may be to his advantage to receive first.

When the winner of the toss has chosen to serve first, the other player must be the receiver and must choose the side from which he will receive. Usually, he elects to receive on the "sunny" side of the court. This permits the server to serve the first game from the "shady" side, but, immediately after the first game when the players change sides and the receiver becomes the server, then he, too, will have the advantage of the sun at his back during his first service game. This well-established *tradition* in which the winner of the toss elects to serve and the receiver then "gives him the good side" leads many beginners (and indeed, many more experienced players as well) to believe erroneously that the winner of the toss gets both serve and side. Such is not the rule, nor is there any unwritten rule which says that the receiver must give the "good" side to his opponent. Strategy, not etiquette, determines the most appropriate choice. In fact, the left-handed player has his own set of guidelines to go by and should study this rule carefully to gain what tactical advantage is available to him.

Delivering the Serve

The Position of the Server   The server must stand with both feet *behind* (not on) the baseline and within the imaginary extensions of the center mark and the singles sideline. When playing singles, the server may not stand behind the doubles alley. Essentially, the server's position is supposed to be a stationary one until after his racket has contacted the ball. Thus, the rules (6 and 7) specify that he may not change his location by walking or running, although slight movements of the feet during delivery are permissible.

Violation of the foot fault rule is probably the most common violation of the rules and one of the most annoying, especially in matches without an umpire, since it is considered a breach of etiquette to call foot faults on your opponent. Even when an umpire is present, this rule is frequently not enforced, so the responsibility for its observation rests almost totally on each individual player. The rule is very simple; the server is supposed to remain in a stationary position behind the baseline, not touching it at all with any part of his foot, until after his racket has contacted the ball. Note that the rear foot may swing over the baseline before the ball is struck providing that it does not touch the baseline or the court. Immediately after contact, the server may put either one or both feet on or over the line into the court.

If you learn to perform the serve legally in the beginning, you will have no bad habits to break, and you will never be faced with the unnerving call of "Foot Fault!" on a crucial point, nor will you be faced with the arguments, accusations, and controversy that seem to surround players who serve illegally.

The Delivery Itself   The rule (6) states that the server, after assuming the previously described position, must toss the ball into the air and strike it before it hits the ground. The delivery is completed when the racket contacts the ball. Note that nothing is said about the manner in which the ball must be hit. Overhand, sidearm, or underhand motions are all legal (providing the ball is hit before it bounces), but, of course, the overhead pattern is by far the most effective.

Beginners (and even some advanced players), in preparing to serve, occasionally toss the ball very poorly. If you do not attempt to hit such a bad toss, it does not count against you, and you may toss the ball again (9). However, if you swing at the ball and miss, you have committed a fault. Since there is no penalty for *not* striking at a poorly tossed ball, the server should refrain from attempting to hit it. There is no limit to the number of times a player may toss the ball before he must hit it, although it is distracting to your opponent and a breach of etiquette if it happens too often.

Alternating Courts (8)   The server begins each game from the right of the center mark and serves to the diagonally opposite service court. The second point is started from the left of the center mark, and the server serves to the receiver's left service court, and so on, in alternating service courts until the game is finished. Whenever an even number of points has been played in a game, that is none, two, four, or any even number, the next point is started in the right court which is also sometimes called the even court. Whenever an uneven number of points has been played in a game, that is one, three, five, seven, or any odd number, the next point is started in the left court or the odd court.

Occasionally, a player will inadvertently serve from the wrong half of the court. If this should happen to you, remember that *all points played stand,* and you simply correct your position. In other words, the score stands but the inaccuracy of the server's station is corrected (10).

Faults   On each point, the server has two chances to hit the ball over the net so that it will bounce within boundaries (liners are good) of the diagonally opposite service court. A serve that is not good is called a fault. If the first serve is a fault, the server tries again, but if the second serve is also a fault, the server has committed a *double fault* and loses the point. The following list summarizes the ways in which a fault can occur (9).

1. The server commits a foot fault, either by assuming an illegal position or by touching the baseline before contacting the ball.
2. The server delivers the serve in an illegal manner.
3. The server misses the ball while attempting to strike it.
4. The served ball does not land within the proper service court.
5. The served ball touches a permanent fixture other than the net (such as a net post, the umpire's stand, the fence, the overhead lights) before it touches the ground.
6. In doubles, the served ball hits the server's partner (ouch!) or anything the partner wears or carries (37).

Let   The service is a let if it touches the top of the net and is otherwise good (13); that is, besides touching the net, it must be legally served, it must go over the net, and it must land within the proper service court (or on a line bounding that court). Note that a served ball which hits the net, goes over the net, and lands outside the proper service, for example, in the alley, in the backcourt, or in the other service court, is a fault. There is no limit to the number of lets that can occur. Any served ball meeting the above definition is a let and must be served over. The service is also a let if the receiver is not ready when the serve is delivered (13). Thus, the server should be sure that the receiver is in position before beginning to serve.

If a player is unable to play a shot because of circumstances beyond his control, for instance, interference due to a ball from another court or to a spectator who suddenly moves into his way, that player may claim a let (12).

When a let is related only to a service, that one service is replayed. When a let is called to provide for an interruption of play, the entire point should be replayed. For example, when the second service is *interrupted* by a ball from another court, upon resuming play, the server is entitled to two serves (12, 23).

Receiving the Serve

Although the position of the server must meet certain specifications, the receiver may stand in any position he desires. He may be on, in front of, or behind the baseline and on, inside of, or outside of the sideline or the center mark and their imaginary extensions (4). Strategy and skill, not rule, dictate the position of the receiver.

The receiver must allow the serve to bounce before attempting to return it, and the ball must be played before it bounces twice. The server wins the point if the receiver touches a served ball (other than a let) before the ball touches the ground (16).

The receiver must be ready when the serve is delivered. The server must wait until the receiver is ready for the second service as well as the first. If the receiver claims to be not ready and makes *no* attempt to return a service, the service is a let and that particular serve must be served again. If the receiver attempts to return the ball, he may not then claim that he was not ready (11). However, the receiver should not stall or delay the play unnecessarily. He is entitled to clear his court of the first serve if that serve was a fault, but he is not supposed to distract the server unduly. Insofar as possible, the server is entitled to two serves in succession.

After the Serve

A player loses the point if (18):
1.   The ball bounces twice on his side of the net.
2.   He fails to return the ball into his opponent's court.
3.   He returns a ball which hits a permanent fixture, such as the umpire's stand, before it *hits the ground*. However, if you hit a return that bounces within your opponent's court and then hits a permanent fixture, such as the side fence, *before your opponent can hit it*, then you win the point (21).
4.   He touches the ball before it bounces, or volleys it and fails to make a good return, even if he is standing outside of his court. This applies to the receiver who catches a serve before it bounces, or to the receiver's partner in doubles, who may be hit by a serve before the bounce, and in both instances, the receiver loses the point unless the serve is a let (37). Although the language is somewhat complex, the intent of the rules is clear and simple. You cannot call a ball out until after the ball has *touched the ground* outside the boundary lines of your court.
5.   He hits the ball more than once in making a shot. The ball must be hit only once and may not be thrown off the racket. Wood shots, however, are legal (and may be very effective!)
6.   He, his racket, or his clothing touch any part of the net while the ball is in play.
7.   He hits the ball before it crosses the net. However, you may contact the ball on your side of the net and permit your racket to follow-through across

the net, providing you do not touch the net (22). The one exception to the rule against reaching over the net to hit the ball occurs if a ball in play bounces within the proper court on your side of the net and rebounds (because of the backspin placed on it) or is blown back over the net onto your opponent's side. In this case, you *must* touch the ball or you will lose the point, and you may, if you have to, reach over the net, without touching it, to do so (22).

8. He permits a ball in play to touch him, or anything he wears or carries, except his racket. Thus, if you run back under a high lob and the ball barely touches your clothing on its way down to the court, you lose the point.

9. He throws his racket at and hits the ball, even if he makes a return that is otherwise good.

10. He *deliberately* commits any act which hinders his opponent in making a shot. If, however, the action which caused the interference was accidental, a let should be called and the point replayed (19, 23).

It is a good return if (22):

1. A ball lands on a boundary line, even on the outside edge of the line. The lines are considered to be part of the court which they identify, and a ball is not out unless it lands *completely outside* the line. In addition, an unwritten rule dictates than on any close ball, you give your opponent the benefit of the doubt.

2. The ball touches the net as it passes over, provided that it then lands in the proper court. Note that, when this happens on a service, the serve is a let, but when it happens during a rally, the ball is in play.

3. The ball is returned outside the net posts either above or *below* the level of the top of the net, even if it touches the post, provided that it then bounces in the proper court.

4. A ball in play strikes a ball left lying on the court. The player must return the ball in play or lose the point. This particular situation could occur only through carelessness or laziness, since balls should not be left lying on the court. In championship play, ball boys clear stray balls before each serve is delivered. If you are acting as your own ball boy, pick up all balls before each point is started, and, if the first serve is a fault, clear it quickly. Three balls are sufficient for a match, and extra balls should be left on the bench.

Scoring

Tennis has its own peculiar scoring system (24, 25) which is quite different from those used in other sports. A contest or match in tennis is based on three units of scoring: points, games, and sets. A player must win at least four points to win a game, at least six games to win a set, and at least two sets to win the match. Thus, the minimum number of points in a match is 48, but in tennis, each point won by a player is called by its own name, not by the cumulative number of points that have been won. If you have no points, your score is called *love*; if you have one point, your score is *15*; if you have two points, your score is *30*; if you have three points, your score is *40*; and if you win the fourth point, you win the *game*.

If each player has won three points, you would expect the score to be called

40-40 or 40 all, but such is not the case. This score is correctly called *deuce*, and one player must now win two consecutive points in order to win the game. The first point after deuce is called *advantage*: advantage in (ad in) if the server wins the point, or advantage out (ad out) if the receiver wins the point. If you have the *advantage* and you win the next point, you have won two consecutive points and you win the game, but if you lose the next point, the score is again called *deuce*.

Although the *rules* do not specify whose score is called first, the unwritten rules and the umpire's manual insist that the server's score is always called first. And indeed, to do otherwise and call the receiver's score first is grossly misleading. Most players will notice the considerable difference between 15-40 and 40-15!

To win a game, you must have won four points, and you must be at least two points ahead of your opponent. To win a set, you must have won six games and be at least two games ahead of your opponent. Thus, you have not won the set if the score is 6-5. If you win the next game, you win the set 7-5, but if you lose the next game and the score becomes 6 all, it looks like a long afternoon! (For an explanation of the new tie-breaker scoring rules, see p. 55.) Fortunately, you don't have to be two sets ahead of your opponent to win the match. In a best of three sets match, you need to win just two sets—any two will do!

Most matches consist of two out of three sets, but in major championship tournaments, men's matches are usually three out of five sets. To win a best of five sets match, you must win three sets. The maximum number of sets in a match for men is five and for women three (27). This and the rule specifying rest periods (30) are the only rules that provide different conditions of play for men and women.

Changing Sides

Players change sides of the court after the first, third, and every subsequent odd game of each set. If the first set ends after an even number of games have been played (for example, 6-2), the players remain on the same side until after the first game of the second set. If the first set ends after an uneven number of games have been played (for example, 6-3), players change sides, play one game, and change sides again (26). This rule is intended to equalize adverse or advantageous playing conditions, such as sun, shade, wind, background, and the like.

Continuous Play

The rule states that "play shall be continuous from the first service till the match be concluded" (30). This rule is not a crucial one for the beginner. It applies primarily to tournament play, and its intent is to reward the player in the most fit condition. It permits a ten-minute rest after the third set (in a best of five sets match) or after the second set when women or juniors are competing. Stalling or resting between points, games, or when changing sides is supposed to be penalized, but the lengthy interpretation and explanation that always accompanies a statement of this rule illustrate both the complexity of the situation and the difficulties encountered in attempts to enforce it. Recent-

What is the score:	
If the server has won	And the receiver has won
No points	1 point
2 points	No points
3 points	1 point
3 points	2 points
1 point	1 point
3 points	3 points
4 points	3 points
4 points	4 points
4 points	5 points
4 points	6 points

ly, the ILTF adopted an interpretation which limits players to twenty seconds when changing sides. The rule is, of course, completely unenforceable in a match played without an umpire. Since most players will rarely have an umpire, each player must assume responsibility for his own conscientious interpretation of the rule and for his subsequent behavior.

A few comments might profitably be addressed to inexperienced or unsophisticated tournament players, especially to those who are on the way to a first tournament. Since "*play* shall be continuous," all warming up and practicing must be done prior to the *first serve of the match*. The social custom of permitting each player to take his practice serves immediately prior to his first service game is in direct contradiction to this rule. Another social custom, that of permitting the server, before the first point of his service game only, to serve until he gets a serve in ("first one in?!"), also disrupts continuous play. You may wish to make some adjustments to this rule in informal play, but please don't let your feelings be hurt, and don't get into an argument if your opponent in a tournament match insists that all practice serves be taken before the match begins. He is absolutely right!

A reasonable interpretation of the continuous play rule permits a player to have a drink of water during the regular changing sides process, but only if water is available at court side. It does not permit a player to saunter outside the court enclosure to the nearest drinking fountain, except during the ten-minute rest period. Occasionally, a mishap involving a player's clothing may be interpreted as being due to circumstances beyond his control, in which case a suspension of play to effect adjustment or repair may be permitted. This particular rule is an excellent example of one which is almost impossible to interpret according to its "letter" alone. However, the "spirit" of the rule is quite clear, and a true sportsman will abide by it.

DOUBLES

All of the above rules apply to doubles as well as singles with the exceptions noted below.

In hitting a forehand drive, do you:
1. Keep your fingers spread slightly on the grip? **V** on the top plate?
2. Start your backswing **early?**
3. Turn your side to the net whenever possible?
4. Shift your weight forward? Use trunk rotation? Hear the "swish"?
5. **Stroke through** the ball without "slugging" or "slapping" it?

The Court

The playing court for doubles is enlarged by the addition of the alleys. The service courts, however, are the same as those used for singles. Note that the server may now take his position behind the doubles alley if he so desires.

Serving in Doubles

The order of service is decided at the beginning of each set, and this order must be maintained throughout the set. Note, however, that the order of service may be changed at the beginning of any subsequent set. Teams must serve alternately throughout the match and partners must alternate serving for their team throughout the set (33). Thus, in a typical doubles match, if your team has won the toss and has chosen to serve, you and your partner decide which one of you will serve first. Usually, this decision is a tactical one, since most doubles teams want the strongest server to serve first. If your team decides to have you serve the first game, your partner must serve the third game. Your opponents must decide to have one partner, again usually the strongest server, serve the second game and the other partner must serve the fourth game.

This order, in which each player serves every fourth game, must be followed throughout the set. However, if you serve out of turn, your partner, who should have been serving, shall serve as soon as the mistake is discovered. All points or faults occurring before the discovery are counted. If a game is completed before the error is discovered, the service order remains as altered for that set (35). The only exception to this rule occurs in the 5 of 9 point tie-breaker game when the service order for one team is altered (consult tie-breaker scoring procedures, p. 55).

The server's partner may take any position on his side of the net, either in or out of the court. Thus, he may, in effect, obstruct the receiver's view of the serve, but note that if the served ball touches the server's partner, it is a fault (34, 37).

Receiving in Doubles

The order of receiving is decided at the beginning of each set, and this order must be maintained throughout the set, but it may be changed at the beginning of any subsequent set. In other words, partners must receive serves throughout the set on the same sides of the court. Thus, if in the first game, you receive in the right court, your partner must receive in the left court. In every game in which you are the receiving team, you must both be in your original positions (34).

The order of serving is *independent* of the order of receiving; that is, the first server for a team is not required to receive in the right court. He may choose either side, but once chosen, he must receive on that side throughout the set.

If an error occurs and your team changes its order of receiving (for example, if your partner inadvertently receives a serve in the right court), the altered receiving order is maintained until the end of the game in which the error was discovered. You and your partner resume your original order of receiving in the next game of the set in which you are the receivers (36).

The receiver's partner also may take any position on his side of the net, but note that if the served ball hits him before it bounces, the serving team wins the point (37).

After the serve and its return by the specified receiver, the ball must be hit alternately by the opposing teams. Thus, either you or your partner, but not both of you, may hit the return into your opponents' court in which case either one of the opponents may return it to your side. Occasionally, on a ball hit down the center between partners, both players will attempt to hit the return. Usually, one player gets there first and hits the ball while the other player hits his partner's racket. Since only one racket actually contacted the ball, this is a legal return.

TIE-BREAKER PROCEDURES

For 1976, the USTA has authorized the use of specific tie-breaking procedures when the score of any set reaches 6 games all. Three methods were approved; the 5 of 9 point "sudden death" method, the 7 of 12 point (the so-called "Wimbledon") method, and the 7 of 13 point method currently being used by WCT. Use of a tie-breaker procedure is permissive, not mandatory, and tournament committees must notify competitors in advance if a tie-breaking procedure will be used. "Sudden death" is the term applied to the 9 point tie-breaker, since, if the score reaches 4 points all, whoever wins the next point wins the set. In the 12 point tie-breaker, if the score is tied at 6 points all, play continues until one player is ahead by 2 points. The 13 point tie-breaker combines features of both systems, but the 13th point decides the set. The 9 point tie-breaker, explained below, is being used extensively. Those seeking further explanation of the 12 point and 13 point procedures should consult the current edition of the USTA Yearbook.

5 of 9 Point Tie-Breaker

In this method, if the score reaches 6 games all, the first player to win 5 points wins the set. If it is your turn to serve, you serve points 1 and 2, from the right and left courts respectively. Your opponent then serves points 3 and 4, from the right and left courts. Players then change ends and you serve point 5 from the right court and, if necessary, point 6 from the left court. Your opponent serves points 7 and 8. If the score is now 4 points all, your opponent serves point 9, from the right or left court as you designate. Allowing the receiver to choose the court in which the deciding point is to be played is intended to equalize somewhat the advantage of being the server. The score of the set is recorded as 7 games to 6. You "stay for one" after a tie-breaker and since you served first in the tie-breaker, your opponent serves first in the next set.

In doubles, the same procedures are used except that each player serves from the same end of the court in the tie-breaker that he has served from during that set. This forces a change in the serving order for one team and thus supersedes USTA rule 33. For example, in a men's doubles match, Al and Bill are playing with Carl and Don. Al and Carl were the first servers for the respective teams. If the score of the set reaches 6 games all, it is Al's turn to serve and he serves points 1 and 2 and Don (note change in service order) serves points 3 and 4. This permits him to serve from the same end of the court from which he has served during the set. Players now change ends of the court and Bill serves point 5 and, if necessary, point 6. If necessary, Carl then serves points 7, 8, and 9. Again, if the score reaches 4 points all, the receiving team has the choice of receiving the ninth, and deciding point, in the right or left court. If this is not the final set of the doubles match, the opponents, either Carl or Don, serve first to start the next set, since Al served first in the tie-breaker game.

Tie-breaking procedures have come into being in an attempt to reduce the length of tennis matches to a format more suitable for spectators. Long-time tennis addicts will recall marathon matches, that seemed to last forever, with set scores of 12-10, 16-14, 20-22, 8-10, and 17-15. Present-day fans can anticipate a conclusion within a much shorter time span. Although players are concerned about the element of chance and the fairness of important matches (and great amounts of money) being won by a single "sudden death" point, spectators seem to be overwhelmingly in favor of the excitement generated by such points. And obviously, tennis promoters, television producers, and tournament directors strongly support the scoring procedures that permit reasonably accurate estimates of the time that will be needed to complete a match. Discussion of the pros and cons of various procedures continues, but undoubtedly some form of tie-breaking procedure will remain a part of tennis in the future.

"NO-AD" SCORING

Another recent innovation in scoring procedures is the "no-ad" system, which is clearly defined by its name. A player must win only 4 points to win the game. Thus, if the score is tied at 3 points all (deuce according to the traditional system), it's game point for both players, since whoever wins the next point wins the game. On the seventh point, the receiver decides whether the serve will be made to the right or left court. No-ad scoring eliminates long deuce-ad, deuce-ad games, again reducing the time required to complete matches. Many intercollegiate events are currently using this scoring system. It is very effective in physical education classes or other situations where time is limited.

The unwritten rules

7

Some unwritten rules of tennis have been mentioned in connection with other topics since they are woven into the fabric of the game. This chapter provides a brief summary of tennis etiquette. Good manners are never out of place. They will help you to meet many tennis friends and to keep them.

Tennis has a tradition of sportsmanship—a tradition that can be exemplified by each player every time he steps on a court. Many people feel that the Golden Rule, "Do unto others as you would have them do unto you," expresses the concept of sportsmanship clearly and simply. Others believe that a thorough understanding and application of the spirit as well as of the letter of the rules is the essence of sportsmanship. However you choose to define this ideal in general, there are specific attitudes and behaviors which characterize the tennis player and spectator who has both good etiquette and good sportsmanship. Practice them now and throughout your tennis career.

Player concentration is essential to top performance; thus, no one should do anything to distract either player. As a player, you make no loud noises while the ball is in play and you avoid mannerisms or movements which may be distracting to your opponent. As a spectator, you should refrain from applauding, from talking, and from moving around until after a point or game is finished. *Quiet, please* is a basic tennis tradition that applies to everyone.

Whenever you set out to play tennis, whether informally for fun and practice or in the more formal tournament and match-play situations, these characteristics will make you a desirable and knowledgeable competitor. You begin to develop them at home as you plan your tennis attire; appropriate clothing is a part of etiquette.

If you make a date to play, be there and be on time. It is particularly poor behavior to break a date or to default unless some real emergency occurs. It is even worse to break a date just because a better opponent happens to come along.

When walking to a court, proceed as quietly as possible outside the fence to the gate that is closest to the court to which you are going. Wait at the gate until the game in progress on the adjacent court is over, and then walk quickly past that court to your assigned court. Never walk onto a court where a point is in progress, even when playing in a social setting at your local school, club, or public park. Always wait until the point is over. In tournament situations, wait until the game is over before crossing an occupied court, and then move fast. If in doubt, wait until the players change sides (you might even have to watch two full games) before you cross a court where a match is in progress. If a tournament match is going on and the only available court is adjacent to it, you should use that court only if your play does not disturb the match. If you wish to carry on a loud conversation with your friendly opponent from one baseline to the other, or if you are so unskillful that you cannot keep your balls on your court, and they continually interrupt the match, you should refrain from using that court until the match is over. You could, of course, use the court to play tennis without the conversation. Perhaps the added attention to your own performance would increase your control of the ball!

Players should assume their fair share of the expense of the balls. Either offer to split the cost of new balls, or, if you play with one other person regularly, take turns bringing the new balls. If you agree to play with used balls, be sure that the ones you offer are in reasonably good condition.

Before you play, greet your opponent in a friendly manner, and, if he is unknown to you, introduce yourself. In a doubles situation, if two opponents know each other, they should take the initiative in introducing their partners to the others. The spin of the racket should be completed before going on the court to warm up. This enables the proper decisions to be made so that both players can warm up on the side on which they will play the first game. It is customary for the two players to check the height of the net at the center using two rackets (fig. 7.1), one standing lengthwise (27″) and the other sideways on

Fig. 7.1
Measuring
the Net

In serving, do you:
1. Use a loose grip until just prior to impact?
2. Release the toss with the fingers as the left arm moves straight up an imaginary pole?
3. Keep the left toes stationary **behind** the baseline?
4. Let the racket head "loop" behind your back?
5. Meet the ball with **full extension** of body and arm?
6. **Hit out,** not down? Follow through **out** after the ball?

---

top of the first one (9"), and to make the necessary adjustments, either in the tension of the net cord or the center strap. As you warm up, try to hit the ball to your opponent so that maximum practice is possible. This is not the match itself, and you're not supposed to be hitting winners or making your opponent run unnecessarily. All warm-ups should be completed before the match begins and all practice serves should be taken by both players before any points are played.

When you are the server, always begin a point with at least two balls in your hand or in your possession. Since play shall be continuous, it is poor behavior to start the point with one ball, serve a fault, spend the next few minutes chasing another ball, and then finally try to put the second serve in play.

The server, according to rule, must wait until the receiver is ready for both the first and the second serve. Beginners, however, are sometimes unaware of this rule and, frequently when the first serve is a fault, will serve the second too quickly for the receiver to get set. If the first serve is a fault, the receiver is entitled to clear the ball from his court, so it will not interfere with the play of the point. He should do this as quickly as possible. Deliberate delay in clearing the serve is distracting to the server, and "quick serving" before the receiver is set is distracting to the receiver. Both acts are contrary to the rules and are breaches of etiquette as well.

Both players should keep score accurately, and the server should announce the score periodically. Knowing the score in an important part of strategy and, in addition, prevents unpleasant disagreements. After each point, collect all balls on your side of the net and return them *directly to* the server, not just anywhere on the server's side of the net. When one of your balls goes astray on an adjacent court, wait until the point in progress on that court is over and then say "Thank you for the ball, please." When a ball from an adjacent court comes onto your court, retrieve it promptly and return it directly to the player requesting it, or roll it gently to the backstop of that court. Some beginners are overly helpful and return a ball, say the first serve which was a fault, to the court from which it came while the players on that court are engrossed in playing out the point which is in progress from the second serve, thus actually interfering with the play. If a ball from another court enters your court in such a manner that your play was interfered with, ask your opponent to play a let. If you win the point and you're not sure whether something may have distracted your opponent, the courteous thing to do is to offer to play a let. If your opponent was truly distracted, he will accept your offer appreciatively, and if not, he will say, "No, thank you, it didn't bother me."

In situations in which there are no officials, you are responsible for officiating on your side of the net. This means that you call your own illegal shots such as double hits, touching the net, reaching over the net, double bounces, and the like. You trust your opponent to do likewise. It is a breach of etiquette to point your finger at him and say accusingly, "You touched the net, you touched the net!" You, not the spectators nor your opponent, are also responsible for calling the balls on your side of the net loudly and clearly. Tennis tradition demands that you give your opponent the benefit of any doubt. A ball hitting any part of the line bounding the proper court is good. If the ball is so close that a call is questionable, play the ball as good. There is nothing wrong with calling out balls out—even if they are close. If you honestly see the ball out, call it out, but you should see the ball out before you call it out. Note that the receiver, not the server, decides whether the serve is good. If the receiver makes no call and returns the ball, the server must be prepared to play it—the server cannot stand there and say "But I thought the serve was out."

In general, if a ball is good, you return it and say *nothing*, and if a ball is out, you call "out," and you do *not* return it. Never make a call until after the ball has bounced. When a ball in play will land very close to a line, you must be prepared to return it if it is good. In fact, you should return it, and if you then see that it has bounced outside the proper court, call "out" *immediately*. Even though you have returned the ball, the bounce of the previous shot takes precedence. Again, you trust your opponent to call the balls on his side of the net. Occasionally, on a sideline call only, you will be in the best position to make a call on your opponent's side of the net. If he asks you "How was it?", you call the ball as you saw it, even though you may have to call your own shot out. If your shot was out, you may tell him it was out even if he doesn't ask you—a true sportsman will do this. If you saw your shot good and he doesn't ask you to make the call, you accept his decision whatever it may be.

Do not talk while the ball is in play. The one exception is in doubles when it is permissible for partners to call "yours" or "mine" to facilitate team play. Partners may also help each other in calling lines and frequently one partner will call "out" or "bounce it" to his partner to aid his partner's judgment. Unnecessary conversation is not welcome between points either, since this distracts both players' attention. Of course, it is a nice gesture to compliment your opponent on his good shots, but do not overdo it to the extent that either of you loses your concentration.

Once a player steps out to play a match, he should not accept coaching from anyone. From this time on, you are on your own, and this is part of the challenge of the game. There is no one to send in signals, to call the plays, or to analyze your opponent's weaknesses for you. It is up to you to figure these things out for yourself. Learn to be self-reliant and ask your friends, parents, and teachers to watch quietly, if they must watch, and to permit you to make and correct your own errors. The only exception to this unwritten rule occurs during some international team competition when the team captain is seated near the umpire's stand and may converse with his team member when the players change sides. During the ten-minute intermission between the second and third sets for women and between the third and fourth sets for men, most players feel that advice and discussion from friends or coaches is permissible since it does not interfere with continuous play.

Your attitude is important. What you say and how you say it are the signposts which others use in assessing you as a future partner, a friendly, congenial opponent, or a "let's not ask him to be a fourth" type. Your opponent is not your enemy. You're both competitors, both wanting to play well, and both trying to raise your game to a high level. This is a joint venture, and there is no room for animosity. If you are not playing well, perhaps your opponent's good playing is the cause of your ineffectiveness. If so, he deserves to be complimented and certainly should not have to tolerate your grumbling about your game. Even if you are both playing badly, griping will not enhance the situation for either of you. Although it is probably impossible to play without some signs of emotion, temperamental outbursts are not considered good etiquette. Learn to control yourself, and you will be in a much better position to control the ball, your opponent, and the outcome of the match.

When playing doubles, it is not only poor etiquette, but it is also poor strategy, to criticize your partner. Obviously, he wants to play well; you do not help him to do so if you constantly nag at him. What he needs most is encouragement or perhaps a gentle reminder to watch the ball or to move his feet. Your complaints about his playing are not necessary. Concentrate on your own play, and perhaps your good shots will take some of the pressure off your partner or may inspire him to play better. It is considered poor form to offer suggestions to your opponent, unless it is a practice match and he has specifically requested that you do so.

Leave the court on which you have played in a neat condition. Throw away empty ball cans, candy wrappers, and such in the nearest trash can, and do not leave trash or dirty towels cluttering the bench or the court.

When others are waiting, do not monopolize the courts. Most courts have rules governing their use posted on the fence or at the entrance. Know these rules and follow them. In some cases, players are permitted to play only one set of singles, but two sets of doubles. Sometimes, players indicate that they are waiting for your court by placing a racket in the fence, which means that at the end of the set, you relinquish it *gracefully*. Frequently, court rules limit the number of games played in a set to 13, so that when the score reaches 7-6, you relinquish the court, even though you haven't finished the set. It goes without saying that you never report the score incorrectly. Some courts are reserved for use by the hour, and when your hour is up, you should leave the court and not hold up other players who have reserved it for the next hour. If the courts are busy, it is your responsibility to share them equitably and according to local rule or custom.

Occasionally, you should offer to play or practice with players of lesser skill. This is particularly helpful to them, and you will be returning a favor that was done for you when you were not as skillful as you are now.

For those of you who wish to experience the added challenges of tournament play, a few additional comments may be helpful. Study the rules and the unwritten rules carefully. Be sure you abide by both sets of guidelines. Read carefully the conditions of play which will be printed upon the tournament's official entry blank. If you do not wish to abide by those conditions, do not enter that tournament. Entries should be filed on time and as directed by the entry blank, usually with entry fees enclosed.

When playing in a tournament, play your best. It is insulting to your opponent to offer him anything less than your best effort, even if you are a much better player. To practice shots and "goof off" when playing a lesser skilled player is extremely bad manners. If you are the lesser skilled player, to quit trying and thereby to offer no competition to your opponent by playing less than your best is equally poor behavior. Treat your opponent with respect, and he will usually return the favor.

If you are playing in a tournament match and linejudges are present, make no line calls at all. Your responsibility is to play, and you return everything until you hear the call "out." The judges assume the responsibility for calling the lines, and you should not dispute the calls. Linejudges do, of course, occasionally make mistakes, and sometimes a judge will change a decision if he believes that he was in error. If the call stands and it went against you, you accept it as part of the game. Occasionally, a player who knows that a linejudge's error awarded him a point that rightfully belongs to his opponent will deliberately lose the next point in a gesture of sportsmanship.

At the conclusion of a match, shake hands with your opponent and thank him for the match. If you lost, congratulate him on his victory and wish him good luck in the next round. Make no excuses for your play, and recognize that your opponent was the better player. If you won, be a gracious winner, console him about his loss and wish him better luck in the next tournament. When an umpire and linejudges have officiated a match for you, thank them for calling the match immediately after its conclusion. When you have concluded your performance in a tournament, you should find and thank the tournament chairman and his committee for their efforts in conducting a well-organized event and for providing you with an enjoyable and educational experience.

Spectators should sit in the area provided for spectators, not on the courtside benches, the fences, or the court surface itself. Only if bleachers are not provided is it permissible for spectators to sit on the courtside benches. Those who choose to do so should be extremely careful to enter and leave the court enclosure when players are changing sides and preferably only at the beginning and end of the match.

Applaud good play after the point is completed, not in the middle of the rally because the player you are rooting for just made a great "get." Even though a spontaneous reaction may be unavoidable, wait until the point is over to applaud. Part of the tradition of tennis is to *applaud only the good shots made by either side* and never to boo the bad shots or the errors. This tradition stresses the positive approach. Applaud the good shots and keep quiet on the errors. This means that you don't applaud if the team you favor wins a point on the other team's error.

If you are interested in the score, keep it yourself, and don't bother the players by continually asking the score. If there is no other way of determining

---

In hitting a backhand drive, do you:
1. Change your grip? First knuckle of the index finger on the top plate?
2. Watch the ball until **after** contact?
3. **Turn** so the **back** of your right shoulder is toward the net?
4. Swing level, or just slightly from low to high?
5. Contact the ball **ahead** of your front foot? Slightly open racket face?
6. Follow through **out** in the direction of the shot?

---

the score, wait until the players change sides, then quietly ask one of them the score. Players, please note that if you would announce the score periodically, spectators would not have to bother you to find out! As a spectator, you are not supposed to coach or kibitz with the players. Their concentration is essential to their performance, and they will thank you to keep still.

Spectators should not act in the capacity of linejudges or umpires. The players are responsible for calling their own lines and should make their own decisions. Rarely is a spectator in good position to make an accurate call on close balls, so even if a player asks, say nothing or tell him that you can't call it. If there are linejudges on the match, it is extremely poor behavior for spectators to "second guess" the linejudge's call. The linejudge is in the best possible position to make the call, and you will do everyone a favor by accepting his decision and by not trying to influence him or to upset the players. He volunteers his services and usually serves without remuneration of any kind. There is no reason for him to be subjected to any kind of abuse. If you wish to improve what you consider to be a poor situation, learn how to call lines—it's not hard—and volunteer your services; then, the lines will be called to your satisfaction!

Both on and off the courts, you will find that courteous manners and sportsmanlike behavior contribute to everyone's enjoyment of the game as well as to the great tennis tradition itself.

The language and lore of tennis

8

To provide a taste and some of the flavor of the game, included here is a descriptive list of some of the more interesting words, the aim of which is to whet your appetite and to spur you on to further study. The list of selected references (p. 82) includes several books and periodicals which will be helpful to you. In general, this chapter contains those terms which have not been described elsewhere in the book. Where duplication does occur, the brief definitions presented here are supplemented by references to the chapter/s in which further information may be found (the numbers in parentheses).

Ace. A good service, served so well that the receiver cannot touch it.

American Twist. An advanced serve in which the racket strikes the ball with an upward and sideward motion causing the ball to spin during its flight and to take a high bounce, usually to the receiver's backhand (3).

Approach Shot. The type of shot behind which a player advances to the net position, usually one hit deep into the opponent's court with medium speed (5).

ATP. Association of Tennis Professionals. An organization of male professional tennis players.

Backspin. Spin applied to the ball by hitting down behind it causing the ball to spin in the opposite direction from its flight (3).

Baseline Game. A type of strategy employed by a player who remains near his own baseline and attempts to outsteady his opponent (5).

Break Point. The point, which if won by the receiver, breaks the opponent's serve, and is a very important point for both players. See Service Break.

Bye. A term commonly used in single elimination tournaments to indicate that a player does not have to play in the first round. The number of byes is determined by subtracting the number of entries from the next higher power of two. USTA tournament regulations prescribe the location of the byes in the draw.

Challenge Round. The last round of a challenge-type tournament. The Davis Cup has been the primary example of this type of tournament in which the champion nation of the preceding year waited while all of the challenging nations played a series of elimination tournaments. The winner of the elimination tournament became the challenger and played the champion in the *challenge round*. In 1972, the Davis Cup format changed to a single elimination tournament.

Chip.   A term applied to short, angled shots, mostly sliced returns of serve in doubles (3).

Chop.   A stroke in which the racket is drawn down and under the ball imparting backspin to it (3).

Consolation Tournament.   Held in connection with a single elimination tournament for first round (sometimes first and second round) losers (10).

Continental Grip.   Sometimes called the service grip. Players who use this grip usually do not change grips for the forehand and backhand drives, but use this one grip to hit all shots (2, 3).

Davis Cup.   A large silver trophy donated by Dwight Davis in 1900. Originally, the trophy was presented to the winner of a series of men's team matches between the United States and England. Now, between 30 and 35 nations compete for the Davis Cup each year. Each team match (called a tie) follows a prescribed format of two singles matches on the first day, a doubles match on the second day, and two more singles matches on the third day. A nation must win three of the five matches to defeat its opposing nation. Each individual match is the best of five sets. See Challenge Round. Davis Cup competition begins early in the year and often is not completed until December.

Dead Ball.   A ball which has lost air pressure and consequently does not rebound as well as a normal or live ball. Poor stroke habits may result from using dead balls (1, 9).

Deep.   A term used to describe a shot that lands within the court near the baseline. A deep serve is one that lands within the service court near the service line (5).

Default.   A player who fails to play a tournament match loses by default, and his opponent moves into the next round.

Dink.   To hit the ball with an extreme margin of error, usually quite high over the net, and quite deep into the opponent's court at a moderate or low rate of speed. This type of player is often called a retriever and relies on his own ability to get the ball back often enough so that his opponent will eventually make an error (5).

Double Elimination Tournament.   A type of tournament in which a player must lose two matches before he is eliminated from the tournament.

Double Fault.   Loss of a point by the server for failing to make good on either of his two chances to serve (6).

Draw.   The organization of competitors in a tournament; in the typical single elimination tournament, each entrant's name is placed on a separate card, and the cards are then drawn at random. The names are entered on the tournament chart in the order drawn (except for the seeded entrants). You may hear discussion about *attending the draw*—the meeting at which the committee actually draws the names from the hat. In fact, you ought to attend a draw sometime —it's very interesting. You may also hear players asking one another *"Have you seen the draw?"* and in this case they are referring to the posted tournament chart listing the entrants in the order drawn. Players will also talk about the *"luck of the draw"* referring to the quality of the opposing players drawn into their quarter or half of the tournament. A player with a "tough" draw must meet a high-caliber opponent in an early round, while a player with a "good" draw meets opponents who are less well known and against whom he has a good chance of winning.

Drive.   Usually refers to a ball hit after the bounce with a full stroke so that it travels fairly fast from one end of the court to the other (2).

Dropshot.   A ball hit softly with backspin so that it just clears the net and lands close to the net with a low bounce (3, 5).

Drop Volley.   Very similar to the dropshot but executed as a volley instead of a groundstroke (3, 5).

Earned Point.   A point won by skillful playing rather than through an opponent's error (5).

Eastern Grip.   The forehand and backhand grips as presented (2).

Error.   A point lost through a mistake not caused by your opponent (5). There are basically two ways in which a point can be won: Either you play so well and hit such an unbeatable shot that your opponent couldn't be expected to make a return, or you play poorly or carelessly and miss a return that normally could be made. The experts say that many more points are lost on errors than are won on placements or on earned points.

Even Court.   The right court since, whenever play is started in this court, an even number of points has been played in the current game (6). Note that the two right service courts are diagonally opposite each other (1).

Face.   The strings of the racket which are the hitting surface (1). A closed face refers to the angle of the racket face when the top edge is turned forward so that the hitting surface faces down toward the ground. An open face refers to the angle of the racket face when the top edge is turned backward so that the hitting surface faces up toward the sky (2). Also see Flat.

Fault.   A technical term indicating an illegal return or serve; much more commonly used to indicate a serve that lands outside of the proper service court (6).

Federation Cup.   International team competition for women which was started in 1963 by the ILTF. A single elimination team tournament is held over a period of four or five days, usually in conjunction with another major tournament. Two singles matches and one doubles match constitute a team match and the nation that wins at least two of the three matches advances to the next round of the tournament.

Fifteen.   Term used in scoring to indicate the first point won by a player in each game (6). The origin of this term is based on early scoring systems in which a player had to make 15 chases to win one point.

Finals.   The last or final round of a single elimination tournament in which two players in a singles event or two teams in a doubles event compete for the championship.

Flat.   Flat face is a term used to describe the position of the racket head when the face is perpendicular to the court and faces the net squarely, sometimes called a square face. A flat drive is produced with a flat face and a level swing thus directing the ball in a fairly straight trajectory with little arc and little or no spin. The term flat is also used to describe a serve hit with no spin (2, 3, 5).

Foot Fault.   A violation of the service rule, usually occurring when a player steps on or over the baseline, although illegal movement of the feet is also a foot fault (6).

Forcing Shot.   A strong attacking shot, usually fast, deep, and well placed, designed to force either an error or a weak return from your opponent (5).

Grand Prix.   A high prize money, combination round robin, single elimination tournament for the top eight male point winners on the year-long Commercial Union circuit.

Grand Slam.   Winning in the same year what some experts consider to be the four major tennis events in the world, the Championships of Australia, France, England (Wimbledon), and the United States (Forest Hills). Don Budge, Maureen Connolly, Rod Laver (twice), and Margaret Court are the only players to have accomplished this feat.

Groundstroke.   A stroke, usually the forehand or backhand drive, used to hit a ball after it has bounced (2).

Half-Volley.   A defensive stroke used to hit the ball immediately after it has bounced. Usually, a player is forced to hit a half-volley because he has not been able to reach a position in the forecourt from which he can make a volley, a much stronger shot (3).

Head.   The frame and strings of the racket (1). Also, that part of the anatomy which many players neglect to use! (5)

Hold Service.   When the server wins the game. If you hold your serve every time, you cannot lose a set (5, 6).

ILTF.   The International Lawn Tennis Federation (1, 6).

Left Court (Player).   The partner of a doubles team who receives service in the left court. The left court is also referred to as the odd court or the backhand court, since usually the player with the stronger backhand plays the left court.

Let.   A serve which hits the top of the net but is otherwise good. A let serve is re-served. Also, a point that is interrupted by interference in which case the point is played over (6).

Lob.   A ball hit so that its flight goes high into the air (usually over the reach of the net player) and deep in the opponent's backcourt. A *lob volley* has a similar trajectory but is hit before the ball has bounced and is considered to be a very advanced and very delicate shot (3, 5).

Loop.   Refers to balls hit with topspin because the flight of the ball seems to dip sharply; also used to refer to players who stroke the ball with a "loopy," as contrasted with a level, swing (2).

Love.   Term used in scoring to mean zero or nothing. This word probably came from the French word "l'oueff" which means goose egg, and when the game was taken to England, the French word was pronounced like "love." A *love game* is won without the loss of a point, and if you win a *love set*, you have won six games, and your opponent has won none. When someone tells you that he has won a match "love and love," his opponent did not win a game (6).

Match Point.   The point which, if won by the player who is ahead, wins the match. A tenacious player might fight off match points held by his opponent and hang on to win the match himself.

Mixed Doubles.   A type of competition in which a man and woman play as partners against another doubles team also so composed.

Net Game.   A type of strategy employed by a player who attempts to reach a position in the forecourt in order to utilize volleys and overheads to win points (5).

Netman (Net Player).   Usually used in doubles to refer to the partner of the server who plays near the net (5).

No Man's Land.   The mid-court area in which a player is particularly vulnerable because so many balls will bounce at his feet forcing him to attempt difficult half-volleys (3, 5).

Not Up.   Refers to a double bounce. This term is used by an umpire when a player fails to play the ball before the second bounce.

Odd Court.   The left court since, whenever play is started in this court, an odd number of points has been played in the current game (6).

On the Rise.   The term used to describe an aggressive style of play in which a player returns the ball before it reaches the height of its bounce. By playing the ball early or on the rise, you give your opponent less time to get set for your return. This style of play is usually not advocated for beginners (2, 5).

Opening.   An offensive opportunity, created either by your own forcing play or by your opponent's errors, which, if utilized properly, should reward you with a point (5).

Overhead Smash.   The advanced shot that is the answer to the lob. The stroke resembles the serve and is a hard overhead swing. It is sometimes referred to as a smash or as an overhead (3, 5).

Overspin.   See Topspin.

Passing Shot.   To hit the ball past the reach of a net player either down the line or crosscourt. One of the choices available to the backcourt player when his opponent rushes the net (5).

Poach.   An advanced technique used in doubles play when the net player leaves his position, crosses in front of his partner to "steal" a ball that would normally have been played by his partner. Look for this when you're watching the experts play, and note how the backcourt team tries to outguess the net player by lobbing or hitting down the line (5).

Put Away.   A shot, also called a kill or a winner, hit so well that no return is expected. A novice may try to put every ball away, but a more experienced player knows that you have to maneuver your opponent out of position before most put away attempts will be successful (5).

Quarter Finals.   In a single elimination tournament, the round in which eight players remain in singles or eight teams in doubles; also called the round of eight.

Rally.   Describes play after the serve to the conclusion of the point. Also a series of shots in which both players are able to keep the ball in play (5).

Rankings.   At the end of each season, national and sectional associations place tournament players in rank order based upon their tournament performances during the preceding year (9).

Retrieve.   Making a long run to return an opponent's good shot. A retriever is a player whose style of play is primarily defensive; that is, he relies on his ability to run down and return any shot that his opponent may hit and does not attempt to hit put aways or risk the possibility of error himself (5).

Return.   A generalized term applying to a ball hit back to your opponent. Sometimes the term used more specifically to refer to the return of service. Since a player cannot win a match unless he can break his opponent's serve, the return of serve is an extremely important aspect of his game (5).

Right Court (Player).   The partner of a doubles team who receives service in the right court. The right court is also referred to as the even court or the forehand court.

Rough.   Rough and smooth refer to the trimming strings that are wound around the racket strings near the tip and near the throat in such a way that on one hitting surface they feel smooth and on the other hitting surface they feel rough. These terms may be used in tossing a racket at the beginning of a match (6).

Round.   Each round of a single elimination tournament is numbered until play reaches the quarter-final, semifinal, and final rounds. First round play refers to the first matches played; at the end of the first round, half of the players who played are eliminated, and the winners of the first round matches move into the second round where the process is repeated.

Round Robin.   A type of tournament in which each player or team plays every other player or team; the winner is the entry that wins the greatest number of matches (10).

Rush the Net.   A style of play in which a player hits an approach shot and runs toward the net where he will be in a better position to win a point (5).

Seeding.   A process by which the best or ranked entrants in a single elimination tournament are placed in the draw so that they will not meet each other in the early rounds of a tournament. The tournament committee, in effect, predicts the winner and seeds that player number one. The committee guesses who will be the second best player and seeds him number two. Usually, for every eight entries, one player is seeded. The seeded players are then placed in specified positions in the draw. If the committee's predictions come true, the number one and number two seeded players will meet in the finals, and they will have defeated the number three and number four seeded players in the semifinals. Seedings are based on rankings and upon recent tournament performance. When a seeded player is defeated by an unseeded player, an upset has occurred.

Semifinals.   In a single elimination tournament, the round in which four players remain in singles or four teams in doubles; also called the round of four. The winners of the two semifinal matches advance to the finals.

Service.   The served ball itself. Also referred to as a serve. Since the receiver must be ready before the serve is delivered, this term is sometimes used by impatient servers to recall the wandering attention of the receiver. It should *not* be used before each point, since its use implies that the receiver is slow or inattentive (7).

Service Break.   When the server fails to win the game he serves, the receiver breaks his opponent's serve. In order to win a set, you must break serve (5).

Set Point.   The point which, if won by the player who is ahead, wins the set (6).

Short Angle Shot.   A type of shot directed crosscourt toward the junction of your opponent's service line and sideline. It is very useful in maneuvering your opponent out of position (5).

Sidespin.   When the ball spins on a vertical axis "like a top" (3).

Single Elimination Tournament.   The most common type of competition in tennis, where a player is eliminated as soon as he loses one match.

Slice.   When this term is applied to a groundstroke or a volley, the ball is hit with backspin, and when applied to a serve, the ball is hit with sidespin (3).

Smash.   Same as Overhead Smash.

Smooth.   See Rough.

Spin.   When force is applied to the ball off center, the ball will spin (3, 5). Also see Backspin, Chip, Chop, Dropshot, Drop Volley, Loop, Sidespin, Slice, Topspin, Twist.

Stop Volley.   Same as Drop Volley.

Sudden Death.   The 5 of 9 point tie-breaker (6).

Tennis.   Presumably derived from the French verb *tenez*, the imperative of *tenir*, which means to hold, take, or receive. Thus, the name of the game is inherent in the rules which require that the server must hold the attention of the receiver before the serve may be legally delivered (6).

Throat. That part of the racket just below the head. While the word "neck" may seem just as logical to a novice, it is *not* appropriate, and its use marks the user as one unacquainted with proper terminology (1).

Topspin. Spin applied to the ball by hitting up behind it, causing the ball to spin in the same direction as its flight (3).

Toss the Racket (Spin the Racket). At the beginning of a match, a racket is "tossed" so that it lands flat on the ground. Formerly the terms rough and smooth were used in calling the toss, and the winner (and the loser) of the toss make certain choices (6).

Trajectory. Refers to ball flight which is caused by the method of stroke production (2, 3). Understanding various trajectories and their attributes plays an important role in strategy and in making the correct choice of shot (5).

Twist. Usually refers to a type of serve hit with topspin, and is sometimes called the American Twist serve (3).

Two-Step. Step-together-step. A movement commonly used to make small adjustments in position. When moving to the right, make the first step with the right foot, bring the left foot up to it, and then step again on the right foot. This frees the left foot to step forward into the shot. Do the reverse when moving to the left.

Umpire. The official, who is in direct charge of a match, supervises the conduct of the linejudges and the players, announces the score at the conclusion of each point, and performs other duties as described in the USTA Umpire's Manual.

Underspin. Same as Backspin.

Unseeded. A player who is not seeded, thus not favored to win or even to survive the early rounds of play. See Seeding.

USLTA. The United States Lawn Tennis Association, which recently (1975) deleted the word "lawn" from its title. See USTA.

USPTA. The United States Professional Tennis Association. An organization of teaching professionals (1770 certified members) designed to promote ethical standards and sound educational methods in tennis teachers.

USTA. The United States Tennis Association (9). Formerly the USLTA.

Volley. A ball hit before it bounces (2) and an essential part of an attacking game (5).

WCT. World Championship of Tennis. One of the early promoters of modern professional tennis, now a highly competitive prize money circuit for men under contract to WCT.

Western Grip. The method of gripping the racket in which the racket is placed face down on the ground and the player merely picks it up and places the **V** on the back plate. A player who uses this grip hits balls on both his left and right with the same grip and the same face of the racket. The Western grip is said to have originated on the hard-surfaced courts in the west where the surface caused high rebounds which can be hit very effectively with this grip. However, it is most ineffective for low bouncing balls, and, since most of the major tournaments are played on grass courts which tend to produce low rebounds, players with Western grips very rarely appear among those on the championship circuit. Further, the mechanical disadvantages inherent in this grip make it an inappropriate choice (2).

Wightman Cup. In 1919, Mrs. Hazel Hotchkiss Wightman, one of the most remarkable ladies in United States tennis history, donated a cup for international women's team competition. She proposed that competition be along Davis Cup lines and that it be open to all nations, but since considerable expense was involved, actual competition did not begin until 1923 and then only between the United States and England. Five singles matches and two doubles matches constitute a team match. The event is held each year, the site alternating between the United States and Wimbledon. At least four players are required to play the matches on a two-day schedule. The number one and number two singles players exchange singles opponents on the second day of play. The United States has won the Cup thirty-two times and Great Britain six times.

WTA.   Women's Tennis Association. An organization of women professional tennis players designed to improve tournament schedules, conditions of play, prize money, player rankings, and player health and pension plans (9).

WTT.   World Team Tennis. A new (1974) professional tennis league in which teams representing cities compete in a round robin schedule. A team match consists of one set of each of the five standard events, thus involves men and women competing professionally on the same team (9).

Facts for enthusiasts

9

SELECTING AND CARING FOR EQUIPMENT

The manufacture and sale of tennis equipment is a large, competitive business. Some statistical reports claim that tennis is a billion dollar business. The "tennis boom" is a reality as the number of people playing and watching the game continues to rise dramatically. Almost every manufacturer of tennis equipment reports astronomical sale increases over the past few years. While the basic equipment requirements are still a racket and a few tennis balls, the quality and cost of this equipment varies considerably. In addition, the purchaser will be confronted with a wide variety of "essential" accessories and thus must understand the options available in order to obtain equipment which is desirable and in an appropriate price range.

A discussion of clothing and balls has been presented in chapter 1. A "heavy" ball is the best buy. Almost all brands of pressurized balls are sold three to an airtight can at very similar prices, approximately $2.50 a can. "Let the buyer beware" of tennis balls which are packaged in cardboard cylinders and sold for much less. These balls will probably be nearly "dead" even when new. The one exception is the nonpressurized ball which does not need to be packaged in an airtight container. These balls are usually packaged four to a cardboard box and cost approximately $3.00 per box.

Wooden racket frames vary in price from $10 to $50. This range reflects differences in the quality of wood used, the number of laminations in the head of the racket, and the quality of the material used on the grip. While the frame of a high-priced racket may appear to be a single piece of wood, closer inspection will reveal as many as 13 separate strips of wood and fiber (called ply) laminated together into a single unit by a bonding process. Often, a little sticker on the racket head frame will say 8-ply, 11-ply or some other number of ply, but you can count the number of strips for yourself. In general, the greater the number of strips there are, the higher the price of the racket. In addition, the quality of the wood influences the cost. Ash, maple, and several types of synthetic fibers are materials commonly used. The outside strip is usually a hardwood to increase durability. A hardwood, such as maple or beech, is also used to make the throat of the racket. The handle is covered with leather, imitation leather, rubber, or plastic grips. The best rackets use a good grade of leather, which is usually perforated and sometimes has raised ridges built into it to permit better absorption of perspiration from the hand.

Several varieties of metal rackets are now on the market and many companies are continuing experimentation with designs, materials, and production methods. Current designs utilize nickel, chrome-plated special alloy steel or nonferrous alloys in the frame which usually has an open Y-shape throat. A leather grip covers the handle and conventional strings are used, although variations in stringing methods and in string tension may be necessary. Costs range from $35 to $80, including strings. Graphite is one of the newest materials used in racket frame construction. The manufacturers claim that it is designed to deliver the best qualities of both wood and metal. Several companies are producing rackets called composites, which are made of a combination of fiberglass and metal, with prices ranging up to $200. Proponents of the new rackets claim many advantages, such as reduced air resistance, more power with less effort, more "feel," and reduced elbow strain.

Rackets usually have 18 long strings and 21 cross strings. One company has recently increased the number of long strings to 20 and advertises that the denser stringing gives increased "feel" and control. Almost all rackets are strung with gut or nylon, although recently a synthetic gut ($12 to $14), providing the resilience of gut and the durability of nylon, has been placed on the market. Most players prefer gut because it has greater resiliency and thus more snap when the ball is contacted. Gut is available in several degrees of thickness. Some tournament players use 17-gauge gut, the thinnest, least durable, but most resilient; most tournament players use 16-gauge, although 15-gauge is appropriate for the majority of weekend, public park, and club players. Usually, when a player desires gut stringing, it is strung to order at a specific tension which may vary between 50 and 70 pounds. The type of racket should also be considered when selecting string tension. The average player would probably do well to stay between 50 and 60 pounds, since the greater the tension, the more difficult it is to control the ball.

Gut is very susceptible to moisture and sometimes even brief exposure to dampness will cause the strings to swell and snap. Most tournament players carry two, three, or more matched rackets just in case the racket strings break during a match. Since play must be continuous, there can be no intermission while a racket string is being repaired, and playing with a broken string is detrimental both to the racket and to the player's performance! Gut is considerably more expensive ($15 to $20) than nylon ($5 to $10). Nylon is moisture-proof, relatively durable, and quite elastic. It can be strung to a prescribed, but lesser, tension (between 45 and 55 pounds) than gut, but will soon stretch slightly, thus losing its original tension and some of its original snap when the ball is contacted. Nylon is preferred by some topflight players who play a retrieving type of game primarily on slow courts. Most school rackets are strung with nylon since it is adequate for beginners and provides good performance at reasonable cost.

In addition to the above matériel and price considerations, rackets come with varying weights, grip sizes, and balance points. Most rackets weigh between 12 and 15 ounces and are classified as light, medium, or heavy. Lightweight rackets (12 to 13 ounces) are appropriate for children and most girls and women. Medium-weight rackets (13½ to 13¾ ounces) are used by some women and some men, and heavyweight rackets (14 to 15 ounces) are usually used by very strong men. Other things being equal, the heavier the racket is, the greater the force imparted to the ball. The heavier racket is, therefore a more efficient tool than the lighter racket, but only if the player is strong enough to use it correctly. The player who attempts to use a racket too heavy for him is very susceptible to faulty stroke habits, unnecessary fatigue, and general discouragement.

The grip size is determined by measuring the circumference of the grip. People with small hands should choose a smaller grip size (4¼" or 4½"), a medium-sized hand needs about a 4⅝" grip, and a large hand requires 4¾" or 5" grip. To determine the correct size for your hand, hold the racket firmly with the forehand grip (**V** on top plate, fingers spread comfortably). The tip of the second finger should be about even with the knuckle of the thumb (fig. 2.1). If the end of the second finger is even with your thumbnail, the grip is too large, and if the second finger presses into the base of your thumb, the grip is too small.

The balance point of the racket is in the center of its length, 13½ inches from either end. Most rackets are evenly balanced, but baseline players usually prefer a head-heavy racket, while volleyers usually prefer a racket light in the head. Place the balance point of your racket on your index finger to see what kind of balance it has.

Choose a racket with weight and grip size appropriate for your size and strength, string tension appropriate to your skill level, balance point appropriate to your type of game, and quality appropriate to your budget. Many fine hours of tennis can be yours with a carefully selected, appropriate, and relatively inexpensive racket.

The player should use a racket only for the purpose for which it was intended—to hit a tennis ball. The manufacturer did not intend for it to be thrown in any manner, nor did he intend for it to be hit against the fence, the net post, the umpire's stand, or a hard-surfaced court. When not in use, the racket needs to be protected primarily from moisture and from warping. It should be kept in a waterproof cover, which also keeps out the dust, and stored in a racket press where equal pressure can be maintained on all parts of the racket head. It may also be stored on a flat surface (lying on the shelf or on the floor of a closet— someplace where it cannot be stepped on easily) or it may be supported by pegs at its throat. The best way to promote warping is to store the racket standing on its head in the corner of your damp locker or even in the corner of a hot, dry closet. If you treat it well, you will gain many hours of pleasurable tennis from its use.

TENNIS ORGANIZATIONS

The official governing body of tennis in this country is the United States Tennis Association. The USTA is made up of member tennis clubs from throughout the nation. There are no individual memberships as such. You personally do not join the USTA; you join a tennis club, and the club holds a USTA membership. The nation is subdivided into 17 sections, each of which has its own sectional association. Some of the functions of the USTA are listed below.

1. It publishes and distributes the offical rules in the *USTA Official Yearbook*, an annual publication, and it maintains a rules interpretation service. It also publishes a monthly magazine, *Tennis USA*, which is distributed to adult enrollees.

2. It conducts, supervises, and *sanctions* both amateur and professional (prize money) tournaments. Certain standards must be met and tournament regulations followed by the committee of a sanctioned tournament.

3. It establishes the national rankings of United States players on the basis of their participation in sanctioned tournaments, including the major grass court tournaments played at private clubs in the Eastern section, frequently referred to as the "grass court circuit," and the open prize money events.

4. It registers U.S. players, thus any player who wishes to participate in USTA sanctioned events must pay an $8.00 registration fee each year.

5. It represents this nation in the ILTF, the International Lawn Tennis Federation. This organization is responsible for conducting Davis Cup and Federation Cup matches.

6. It operates for this nation the Davis Cup, Federation Cup, and Wightman Cup programs. Selecting, training, and financing the U.S. teams which compete in these international events are the responsibilities of the USTA.

7. It provides many services to the tennis-playing community in general, for example, free and inexpensive materials, film rentals, junior development programs, Junior Wightman Cup and Junior Davis Cup programs for promising younger players, and clinics and workshops for tennis instructors.

8. It establishes rules which determine amateur and professional player status. An amateur is one who has received no monetary gain by playing, teaching, or demonstrating the game, although there are certain exceptions. Some of these are given below.

   a. A touring tennis player is permitted to receive a certain amount of money to defray his expenses. The ILTF specifies a maximum which may be paid to a player.

   b. A student in regular attendance at college may be employed during vacations periods as a camp counselor, a tennis professional's assistant, or a club employee; *however*, pay must be on a weekly or monthly salary basis, not on an hourly or per lesson basis.

   c. Regular members of a school or college faculty are allowed to teach tennis as a part of their faculty assignment, or coach, if they are also a regular member of the faculty.

d. A high school or college student may be the recipient of a scholarship or other benefits provided by the school or college being attended.

Each sectional association is the voice of the USTA for its specific area. The sectional association assists in the formation of clubs, handles the sanctioning of tournaments for the area, supervises the scheduling of tournament dates, determines the sectional rankings of its players and assists its champions to compete in national tournaments, operates junior development programs, handles registration cards for the area, and provides other similar services. Members of the sectional association are also members of the USTA and are the private clubs, colleges, and institutions of the area.

Another type of tennis organization is operated by municipal and county recreation departments. The NPPTA, the National Public Parks Tennis Association, sponsors a national tournament that moves to a different location each year. This tournament carries a USTA sanction but limits participation to public park players, those who do not belong to private clubs.

The United States Professional Tennis Association (USPTA) is an organization of professional tennis teachers. Certified members have demonstrated knowledge of tennis, skill in playing the game, and knowledge of sound teaching methods appropriate for both private and group instruction. In addition to other activities, the USPTA promotes ethical standards among its members and has endorsed a Tennis Academy which gives basic courses for aspiring tennis teachers and advanced courses for members who wish to improve their teaching and business skills.

The Association of Tennis Professionals (ATP) for men and the Women's Tennis Association (WTA) are organizations of professional tennis players, who compete in the prize money tournaments. Members of each of these organizations come from many countries throughout the world. The organization serves as a unifying force and represents the players in their negotiations with tournament promoters.

SPECTATOR TENNIS

Increasing interest in tennis has convinced promoters and advertisers that tennis can help to sell their products. Consequently more companies are sponsoring tennis events both live and on television. In 1974, 192 hours of tennis were telecast nationally by the three major commercial networks and the Public Broadcasting Service. This kind of exposure with the increased opportunity to watch the top players play excellent tennis has served only to further increase the public interest. Today's beginner can watch the experts play exciting points and matches, can listen to commentators discussing the fine points of rule and strategy, and can receive topflight instruction on strokes without setting foot out of the living room.

The latest addition (in 1974) to the spectator market is World Team Tennis (WTT) which features teams composed of both men and women representing various cities across the country. A team tennis match consists of one set of each of the five standard events; men's and women's singles, men's and women's doubles, and mixed doubles. No-ad scoring is used; and the sudden death tie-breaker is played at 6 games all. The number of games won by players representing each team is cumulative, and the match is won by the team winning the greatest number of games in the five sets. The scoreboard at a WTT match might read 3-1, 3-3, and 9-7. This would indicate that one team was leading three points to one in the game being played, that the set score was tied at 3 games all, and that the first team took the first set 6-4, and thus, is leading the team match 9 games to 7. If the teams are tied at the end of the last set (the mixed doubles), a 9 point tie-breaker is played to determine the winner of the team match. Individual players may compete in no more than two of the sets, coaches may put in substitutes, and spectators are encouraged to cheer for their favorite players and applaud the good shots without waiting for the end of the point.

Playing the game

10

Where can you play? There are many different types of facilities for playing tennis, each with its own set of customs and regulations which you will want to follow. Most *high schools and colleges* have their own courts and while these are reserved for class during certain hours, they are usually available to students for extra practice and recreational play when classes are not in session. Since classes do have priority, be sure to leave quickly and graciously when an instructor asks you to do so. If there should be an extra court available, most instructors will be happy to have you continue your game, providing, of course, that you do not distract the class.

Almost all communities provide *public tennis courts* in parks and other recreational areas. These are usually operated by municipal or county recreation departments. Typically, these courts are open to the public, although residents of the particular community may have priority. Some public courts are simply there, and it's first come, first served. Other public courts are operated on a permit basis, and you have to phone or visit the office to secure a permit which may entitle you to play for one or two specified hours. When courts are lighted for night play, the policies regarding their use may differ from those in effect during the day. If you are new in a community, call the local recreation department office and find out what the local policies are. This office can also tell you what kinds of organized tennis programs are being operated and can usually introduce you to the tennis-playing members of the community.

Sometimes, an individual family will have a *private tennis court* in its backyard. You don't play there unless you are invited. The same thing holds for most *private tennis clubs.* You don't play there unless you are a member or unless a member invites you to be his guest. If you would like to join a private club, it is perfectly proper to inquire at the club office about the availability, cost, and eligibility requirements for membership. Most private clubs have several types of memberships, including family, individual, and junior, each with its own set of privileges and charges. Clubs that have multiple facilities, such as, golf, tennis, swimming, and the like, frequently offer memberships for golf alone or tennis alone, and, again, each type of membership will have specified costs and privileges. If you join a private club, abide by the privileges and responsibilities of membership that have been established. The tremendous growth of *indoor court* facilities, especially in wintry climates, has been paralleled by a great increase in the number of tennis participants which a recent U.S. survey has shown to be more than 34 million.

What kind of competition is available? All kinds of competition are available no matter what your age, sex, or skill level. The USTA and many sectional associations sanction tournaments in the following age divisions: 10 and under, 12 and under, 14 and under, 16 and under, 18 and under, 21 and under; open; for men, 35 and over (Junior Veterans), 45 and over (Seniors), 55 and over (Senior Seniors!); and for women, 40 and over (Seniors). Whatever your age, there is a place for you!

There are five standard events in most adult tournaments: Men's Singles, Women's Singles, Men's Doubles, Women's Doubles, and Mixed Doubles. In addition, some enterprising tournament committees run events such as husband-and-wife mixed doubles, father-and-son doubles, mother-and-daughter doubles, father-and-daughter doubles, mother-and-son doubles, and veteran mixed doubles (the combined ages of both players must be 70 or over).

In some parts of the country, "classified" tournaments are held for players of varying skill levels. It works this way: Players are classified A, B, C, and D, with A as the highest classification and D the lowest or novice classification. An A player may enter A events only, but a B player may enter either or both A and B events. Thus, players of a given classification are permitted to play at their own level or at a higher level, but not at a lower level. This gives the beginners, those with little or no tournament experience, a chance to compete with others of comparable ability. In some places, you may enter a D or novice event only once; the next time you enter, you must play a higher classification. Sometimes, you retain your classification until you reach the finals of a tournament at that level, and then, you are automatically reclassified at the next higher level. Classification policies vary considerably, but the idea is to provide lots of action for people of similar skills and experience.

If you are a student, you can get a good start in tournament play by entering your school or college intramural tournament. Drop by the intramural or physical education department office and find out when it will be held, how to enter, and how it operates. Usually, intramural tournaments are of the single elimination type. Once you lose, you're out, but occasionally, especially if the entry is large enough, consolation or double elimination tournaments are organized. In double elimination tournaments, you have to lose twice before you're out, which gives you a chance to recover in case a "bad day" contributed to your first loss. In a consolation event, all the first round (sometimes first and second round) losers are placed in a separate event. This and the classification system described above serve similar purposes.

Many schools and colleges also sponsor tennis teams for men and for women. Interscholastic and intercollegiate team competition can provide a tremendous backlog of match play experience and many very enjoyable friendships. A typical intercollegiate team match consists of six singles matches and three doubles matches. The best players of each team play in the number one singles match, the second-best players play the number two singles match, and so on. Each match is the best two out of three sets, and the winner of each match scores one point for his team. Each coach arranges his team personnel into the three strongest possible doubles combinations and ranks them in order of ability to play against the opposing school's doubles teams. The team winning the greatest number of points wins the match. Usually, colleges within a league or conference play a round robin type of schedule, that is, each college plays every other college to determine the conference standings. In some leagues, players may play singles and doubles, while in others, players may participate in only one event. Sometimes, a team match consists of five singles matches and two doubles matches or four singles matches and three doubles matches. The format varies, but it all adds up to many hours of enjoyable tennis.

Many other opportunities for competitive play exist within your locality. Most communities sponsor a city tennis championship—sometimes two. One is usually a closed tournament and the other an open; thus, only the residents of Podunk can enter the Podunk City Closed, but anyone can enter the Podunk City Open, unless it is restricted to amateurs only. If you belong to a tennis club, it will probably schedule several different types of tournaments throughout the year. A popular type of club tournament is the challenge ladder in which each entrant is assigned or drawn to a rung of the ladder. A player may challenge another player one, two, or three rungs above him. The match is arranged at the convenience of both players, and, if the challenger wins, they trade places on the ladder, otherwise, both players stay in their original positions. There are many variations of the basic ladder tournament, so check the rules which usually can be found posted next to the ladder itself.

Tournaments outside your local area frequently provide concomitant benefits inherent in traveling, in meeting new people, in visiting nearby scenic attractions, and, generally, in enlarging and enriching your own private tennis world. Even the average player can gain from tennis travels to nearby communities and to the state and sectional championships in the area. These tournaments, however, are not appropriate for beginners who should gain the necessary experience on the school, park, and local level. As you go up the tennis ladder, both national and international tournaments may bid for your participation as a competitor. Wimbledon, Forest Hills, the French Championships, the Australian Championships, and major tournaments in many other nations throughout the world beckon those at the highest levels of skill.

Most of the world's high-ranking tennis players will agree that the greatest thrill in tennis is the opportunity to represent your nation in international team competition. The men and women who compete for the Davis Cup, the Wightman Cup, and the Federation Cup will long remember the inner excitement and pride sensed when the umpire announces "game for the United States"!

Additional opportunities for playing the game are available to highly skilled players, who turn professional and subsequently compete for prize money. The development of professional tennis competition has been a fairly recent one, and the touring pros are much more highly organized now than they were formerly. In the past, two, three, or four players toured the country in a long series of exhibition matches, the winner being the player who won the greatest number of matches on the tour. In the early 1970s, World Championship of Tennis (WCT) promoted international tennis competition as a profit-making business venture. Thirty-two of the world's leading male players were under contract to WCT which guaranteed the players a minimum amount of money plus paying air fares to and from the various tournament sites. The contract pros competed for 35 to 45 weeks of the year for prize money which was earned in increasing amounts for each round won. Presumably, the best player was the one who won the most money. In 1971, Rod Laver won more than $200,000.

Increasing pressure for "open" tournaments in which top-ranking amateurs could compete against top-ranking professionals finally resulted in the world's first Open, in England, in April 1968 when one of the amateurs provided considerable excitement as he upset two highly ranked professionals. The women, too, initiated their own pro tour under the sponsorship of World Tennis Magazine and Virginia Slims. Although the money available for prizes was not so great as that for men, the leading female money winner of 1971, Billie Jean King, exceeded her announced goal of earning $100,000 prize money in one year, the first woman in any sport to achieve that goal.

In the few short years since open tennis arrived, the tennis world has seen contract pros, independent pros, Women's Liberation, increasing prize money, the banning of players, the boycotting of tournaments, continuing problems, and some fantastic tennis. Prior to 1968, there were very few playing pros and prize money was minimal, but by 1974, prize money on the various circuits, the WCT, The Commercial Union Grand Prix, and the Virginia Slims tour, was close to $8 million and many players were seeking their share of the gold. More people are playing and watching better tennis than ever before.

This, then, has been a brief introduction to the wonderful world of tennis! Hopefully, the basic information provided here has infected you with enough enthusiasm and excitement to make you a lifetime tennis participant and a permanent member of the tennis-minded community. Beyond the scope of this publication lies a much wider horizon. You can continue to enlarge your own view of the game by watching the experts, both amateurs and professionals; by reading books and periodicals suggested in the list of selected references; by taking group or private lessons from experienced teachers or professionals; by practicing and playing on your own with all kinds of opponents; and by joining and contributing to a local or national tennis organization. You, too, can belong, serve, and enjoy the worldwide game that is tennis today.

Selected references

BOOKS

ASHE, ARTHUR with FRANK DEFORD. *Arthur Ashe: Portrait in Motion*. Boston: Houghton Mifflin Co., 1975.

BARNABY, JOHN. *Advantage Tennis*. Boston: Allyn and Bacon, Inc., 1975.

CUMMINGS, PARKE. *American Tennis*. Boston: Little, Brown and Company, 1957.

GALLWEY, W. TIMOTHY. *The Inner Game of Tennis*. New York: Random House, 1974.

GOULD, DICK. *Tennis Anyone?* 2d ed. Palo Alto: The National Press, 1971.

HARMAN, BOB and KEITH MONROE. *Use Your Head in Tennis*. Rev. ed. New York: Crowell, 1975.

KING, BILLIE JEAN and KIM CHAPIN. *Tennis to Win*. New York: Harper and Row, 1970.

MASON, R. ELAINE. *Tennis*. Boston: Allyn and Bacon, Inc., 1974.

McPHEE, JOHN. *Wimbledon: A Celebration*. New York: The Viking Press, 1972.

MURPHY, BILL. *Complete Book of Championship Tennis Drills*. West Hyack, N.Y.: Parker Publishing Co., Inc., 1975.

MURPHY, BILL and CHET MURPHY. *Tennis for Beginners*. New York: The Ronald Press Co., 1958.

MURPHY, CHET. *Advanced Tennis*. 2d ed. Dubuque, Iowa: Wm. C. Brown Co. Publishers, 1976.

MURPHY, CHET and BILL MURPHY. *Tennis for the Player, Teacher and Coach*. Philadelphia: W. B. Saunders Co., 1975.

NEWCOMBE, JOHN and ANGIE with CLARENCE MABRY. *The Family Tennis Book*. Published by Tennis Magazine with Quadrangle. The New York Times Book Co., 1975.

RAMO, SIMON. *Extraordinary Tennis for the Ordinary Player.* New York: Crown Publishers, Inc., 1970.

TALBERT, BILL with GORDON GREER. *Weekend Tennis.* Garden City, New York: Doubleday and Co., Inc., 1970.

TALBERT, WILLIAM and Editors of Sports Illustrated. *The Sports Illustrated Book of Tennis.* Rev. ed. Philadelphia: J. B. Lippincott Co., 1972.

TALBERT, WILLIAM F. and BRUCE S. OLD. *The Game of Doubles in Tennis.* Philadelphia: J. B. Lippincott Co., 1956.

————. *The Game of Singles in Tennis.* Philadelphia: J. B. Lippincott Co., 1962.

TILMANIS, GUNDARS A. *Advanced Tennis for Coaches, Teachers and Players.* Philadelphia: Lea & Febiger, 1975.

United States Lawn Tennis Association. *Official Encyclopedia of Tennis.* New York: Harper and Row, Publishers, 1972.

United States Tennis Association. *USTA Official Yearbook.* 51 E. 42nd Street, New York, N.Y., 10017.

MAGAZINES

Tennis Illustrated. Published monthly by the Devonshire Publication Co., 630 Shatto Place, Los Angeles, Ca. 90005.

Tennis Industry. Industry Publishers, Inc., 14961 N.E. 6th Ave., North Miami, Fla. 33161.

Tennis: Magazine of the Racquet Sports. Official monthly publication of the USPTA. Published by Tennis Features, Inc., 297 Westport Ave., Norwalk, Conn. 06856.

Tennis USA. Official publication of the USTA. Published monthly by Chilton Co., Chilton Way, Radnor, Pa. 19089.

World Tennis. Published monthly by CBS Publications, the Publishing Division of CBS, Inc., 383 Madison Ave., New York, N.Y. 10017.

Appendix: Tennis knowledge test and answers

Try the test *before* you read the book. You'll know the answers to some questions just based on your past experience in tennis and other sports and your exposure to tennis through the news media and television. Use a separate piece of paper as an answer sheet; then you'll be able to use the test over and over to assess your improvement in knowledge and understanding. Grade your paper by using the answer key on p. 92, and compare your first score with our rating system to see where you stand when you start. *Then* read the book, listen to your instructor, practice the skills, play the game, and try the test again. You'll be pleased with your progress, we hope!

For each question that you miss, review the pages referred to in the parentheses beside the question. And write to us if your interpretation differs from ours! Knowledge of these facts and concepts, especially if you can apply them appropriately, will help you to enjoy your participation in tennis both as a spectator and as a player.

MULTIPLE CHOICE

On a separate sheet of paper, write the letter of the *BEST* answer. Read each question carefully. All questions are written for right-handed players.
1. Which of the following procedures is legal according to the official rules?   (p. 5)
   a. A player must use an officially approved racket.
   b. All tennis rackets must be the same length and width so that the correct height of the net may be easily measured.
   c. A player may play with any implement he desires to use, such as a broom, a squash racket, or a frying pan.
   d. None of these.
2. What is the ready position in which a player should wait for his opponent to return the ball?
   (pp. 7-8)
   a. the weight well back on the heels and the knees straight.
   b. the weight forward on the balls of the feet, the feet slightly apart and the knees bent.
   c. the weight forward on the balls of the feet, the feet close together and the knees straight.
   d. the feet wide apart, the knees bent and the body turned for a forehand drive.

3. In hitting a groundstroke, where should the player have his weight at the moment of impact?   (pp. 11, 14)
   a. on his rear foot.
   b. evenly distributed on both feet.
   c. on his forward foot.
   d. in front of his forward foot.
4. Which of the following actions should be emphasized more than usual when stroking a low-bouncing ball?   (p. 10)
   a. Shorten the backswing.
   b. Shorten the follow-through.
   c. Loop the forward swing.
   d. Bend the knees.
   e. Drop the racket head.
5. Which of the following applies to the volley?   (pp. 19-22)
   a. It requires a long, vigorous forward swing.
   b. It is used primarily from the backcourt.
   c. It is used primarily in the forecourt.
   d. It is most frequently hit with a backhand.
6. In hitting a flat volley, where should the ball be contacted?   (p. 21)
   a. in front of the volleyer and below the level of the net.
   b. behind the volleyer and above the level of the net.
   c. behind the volleyer and as high as possible.
   d. in front of the volleyer and as high as possible.
7. In hitting a backhand drive, what is the most desirable spot to contact the ball? (p. 14)
   a. opposite the rear foot.
   b. just ahead of the rear foot.
   c. opposite the center of the body.
   d. opposite the forward foot.
   e. just ahead of the forward foot.
8. When playing a baseline game, what should the player's position be?   (p. 8)
   a. approximately three feet behind the baseline.
   b. right on the baseline.
   c. between the baseline and the service line.
   d. halfway between the baseline and the net.
9. When serving, why is it desirable to put spin on the ball?   (pp. 23-25)
   a. It causes the ball to bounce in an unexpected manner, thus making it more difficult to return.
   b. It permits greater control of the ball.
   c. It permits a wider margin of error as the ball crosses the net and causes the ball to drop more rapidly within the service court.
   d. All of these.
   e. None of these.
10. When using a lob, generally, where is it most advisable to place the ball?   (p. 43)
    a. near the baseline.
    b. close to the service line.
    c. just over the opponent's head.
    d. to the opponent's backhand.
    e. close to the sideline.
11. What is the primary purpose of the lob?   (pp. 25, 43, 44)
    a. to gain time in order to return to a ready position.
    b. to force the opponent from the net.
    c. to give the player time to go to the net.
    d. all of the above.
    e. statements (a) and (b) above.
12. In serving an American Twist, where should you toss the ball?   (pp. 18, 25)
    a. directly in front of you.
    b. to your left and slightly behind you.
    c. to your right and slightly behind you.
    d. to your right and slightly in front of you.
13. How is underspin applied to a backhand?   (p. 24)
    a. Start with the racket head at a point below ball level, swing up and follow through high.
    b. Turn your wrist over as you hit.
    c. Start with the racket head at a point above ball level, swing down and follow through low.
    d. Tilt the racket backwards so the face is slightly open to the sky.

14. If other things are equal, which of the following will have the greatest speed? A drive hit with (pp. 23-24)
    a. backspin.   b. topspin.   c. sidespin.   d. no spin.
15. What is the advantage of imparting topspin to the ball on a groundstroke? (pp. 23-24)
    a. It allows a player to hit the ball harder since it will dip downward in its flight.
    b. The ball will be more stable in its flight and will slow up on its bounce.
    c. It will bounce lower than will a ball with either backspin or no spin imparted to it.
    d. There is no advantage whatsoever in imparting topspin to a ball.
16. Which of the following shots is good for returning serve in doubles? (p. 42, 65)
    a. a high crosscourt floater.
    b. a short lob to the netman.
    c. a dropshot.
    d. a chip hit crosscourt at the server's feet.
17. If you are at the net, when will your opponent have a good chance to pass you? When your shot bounces (pp. 43-44)
    a. just inside the baseline.
    b. in no man's land.
    c. on the service line.
18. When rushing the net, which of the following is most important in making the first volley? (p. 44)
    a. Hit it on the run in order to get into good net position as quickly as possible.
    b. Run forward, stop and get set, volley, then move forward another few steps.
    c. Run forward, stop and get set, volley, then wait to see where your opponent is going to hit.
19. If you hit a forehand down the line to your opponent's backhand and you follow your shot to the net, where should you stand to anticipate the return? (p. 40)
    a. on the center service line, halfway between the service line and the net.
    b. two or three feet to the right of the center service line.
    c. two or three feet to the left of the center service line.
    d. in the service court, two or three feet from the right alley.
20. What is the usual position of a good player waiting to receive service? (p. 42)
    a. on the service line.
    b. near the baseline, inside the singles sideline.
    c. directly behind the alley.
    d. outside the alley, a step or two nearer to the net than the baseline.
    e. inside the court boundaries.
21. In singles, after each stroke made from the baseline, how should the player position himself? (p. 40)
    a. between the service line and the baseline.
    b. directly behind the center mark.
    c. directly behind the left side of the court.
    d. on a line that bisects the angle of the opponent's possible return.
22. In doubles, when one partner is serving, what is the correct net position for the other partner? (pp. 40-41)
    a. one foot from the net.
    b. three to five feet from the net.
    c. five to eight feet from the net.
    d. ten to twelve feet from the net.
23. Which of the following is the most important factor in doubles strategy? (p. 44)
    a. the ability to approach and hold the net position.
    b. good smashing ability by both partners.
    c. good speed by at least one partner.
    d. skill in lobbing.
    e. control of the backcourt.
24. On the second serve, the server serves underhand into the proper service court, and the receiver makes no effort to return it, claiming that the serve was delivered incorrectly. What is the ruling? (p. 48)
    a. The server wins the point.   c. A let is called and the ball is re-served.
    b. The receiver wins the point.   d. The point is replayed.

25. What choice is given the winner of the toss? (p. 47)
    a. sides of the court.
    b. serving or receiving.
    c. serving, receiving, or sides of the court.
    d. the number of games to be played in each set.
    e. serve and side, or receiving.
26. The server serves before the receiver is ready and the receiver does not attempt to return the serve. What is the decision? (p. 50)
    a. A fault is called.
    b. A let is called.
    c. A point is awarded to the server.
    d. A point is awarded to the receiver.
27. What is the decision when the server tosses the ball up and catches it instead of striking at it? (p. 48)
    a. A fault should be called.
    b. A let should be called.
    c. The server may try again without penalty.
    d. The server may try again, but if the same action is repeated, a fault occurs.
28. Which of the following is a foot fault? (p. 48)
    a. The server steps over the baseline just before the served ball crosses the net.
    b. The server steps over the baseline before his racket strikes the ball.
    c. The server's feet are both off the ground when the ball is struck.
    d. None of these.
29. Where should the service be made when the score is 40-love? (p. 49, 51)
    a. from the right side of the court.
    b. from the left side of the court.
    c. from either side, depending upon the side from which the game was started.
    d. from either side, depending upon the side from which the last service was made.
30. When is a ball considered out? When it hits (p. 51)
    a. completely behind the line.
    b. just the back edge of the line.
    c. more off than on the line.
    d. any part of the line.
    e. completely in front of the line.
31. In doubles, where must the server's partner stand? (p. 54)
    a. anywhere in his own half of the serving court.
    b. anywhere on the server's side of the net providing that he does not obstruct the view of any player.
    c. anywhere on his side of the net if he is within the court boundaries.
    d. anywhere on his side of the net regardless of boundaries or other players.
32. In a doubles game, on the second serve, the server serves the ball which hits the net cord and then drops into the receiver's alley. The receiver cannot reach it in time to return it. What is the ruling? (p. 49)
    a. The serve is a let.
    b. The serve is a fault.
    c. The server wins the point.
    d. The server loses the point.
33. In the first game of a doubles match, player A received serve in the right-hand court and his partner, player B, received serve in the left-hand court. In the second game, when they serve, which partner must serve? (p. 55)
    a. Since player A receiver serve in the right court, he must be his team's first server.
    b. Since player A was the first receiver, he must be the first server.
    c. Since player B was the second receiver, he must be the first server.
    d. Since the order of serving and the order of receiving are independent of each other, either partner may serve first.
34. Which of the following is *not* a good return? (pp. 50-51)
    a. The ball passes outside the net post and lands in the court.
    b. The player follows through over the net.
    c. The player reaches over the net to play a ball which has bounced back over the net before he reached it.
    d. The player volleys a ball before it passes the net.
    e. All of these.

35. What is the score when the receiver wins the next point after deuce?   (p. 52)
    a. game for the receiver.
    b. 40-30.
    c. 30-40.
    d. advantage in.
    e. advantage out.
36. Using the traditional scoring system, when is a game completed?   (pp. 51-52)
    a. when one side has won four points and the opponents have not more than two points.
    b. when one side has won four points and the opponents have won three.
    c. when a total of four points has been played.
    d. when either side wins five points.
37. Which of the following scores is a completed set?   (p. 52)
    a. 4-2.   b. 6-5.   c. 9-8.   d. 8-6.   e. 5-1.
38. Player A's first serve is a fault. After the second serve, which is good, a dog runs across the court, interfering with the opponent, player B. What is the decision?   (pp. 49-50)
    a. The point is awarded to player B because of the interference.
    b. The play continues.
    c. The second serve must be re-served.
    d. The whole point is replayed and two serves are allowed the server.
39. During play, the server struck at a ball and missed it; the ball landed outside the baseline. What is the ruling?   (pp. 50-51)
    a. point for the serving side.
    b. point for the receiving side.
    c. let.
    d. fault.
    e. legal, the ball remains in play.
40. The score is 15-30. By error, the server serves from the right half of the court and delivers a fault. The error is then discovered. What is the score and where should the server stand to deliver the next serve?   (p. 49)
    a. 15-40, no faults, right court.
    b. 15-30, one fault, right court.
    c. 15-40, one fault, left court.
    d. 15-30, one fault, left court.
41. A player throws his racket at the ball, the ball hits the racket and rebounds over the net into the court. What is the ruling?   (pp. 50-51)
    a. The point is replayed.
    b. The player wins the point.
    c. The opponent wins the point.
    d. The ball continues in play.
42. When may a doubles team change its order of serving?   (p. 54)
    a. at the beginning of any game in a set.
    b. at anytime during the match.
    c. at the beginning of any set.
    d. the serving order may not be changed.
43. In doubles, when may the order of receiving be altered?   (p. 54)
    a. at anytime during the match.
    b. when the service changes.
    c. when the teams change sides of the court.
    d. when the next set starts.
    e. never; the receiving order may not be changed.
44. A doubles team changes its order of receiving by mistake and it is not discovered until the score is 15-love. What is the decision?   (p. 55)
    a. Players switch immediately to reestablish the proper order.
    b. Players switch at the beginning of the next game in which they are the receivers to reestablish the proper order.
    c. The reversed order is continued until the end of the set.
    d. The reversed order is continued until the end of the match.

45. Player A is serving in a doubles game between players A and B and players C and K. The score is 30-15 and one fault has been served when it is discovered that player B should have been serving. Which of the following procedures is correct? (p. 54)
    a. The score remains at 30-15, one fault, and player A continues serving the rest of the game.
    b. The score remains at 30-15, one fault, and player B serves the rest of the game.
    c. The score becomes 30 all and player A continues to serve the rest of the game.
    d. The score becomes 30 all and player B serves the rest of the game.
    e. None of the above answers are correct; the correct procedure is (you describe it).
46. If the opponents lob to your partner who has a very bad overhead, what should you do? (p. 60)
    a. Encourage him by calling out "Hit it!"
    b. Groan loudly "Oh no, not again!"
    c. Push him out of the way and holler "Mine!"
    d. Say nothing.
47. What should the receiver do if he is unable to determine whether a ball is good or just outside? (p. 60)
    a. Call a fault.
    b. Ask the server to make the decision.
    c. Call the ball good.
    d. Ask the server to play the point over.
48. What is the best procedure when one of your balls rolls onto a neighboring court where play is going on? (p. 59)
    a. Call to a player on that court to return the ball.
    b. Run onto the court and get it out of the way quickly.
    c. Wait until the point is finished on the neighboring court and then ask for it.
    d. Consider it a lost ball which should not be recovered at all.
49. What does it mean when a player receives a "bye" in a tournament? (p. 64)
    a. He is placed against an easy opponent.
    b. He is eliminated from the tournament.
    c. He is advanced to the next round of the tournament.
    d. He is privileged to select his first round opponent.
50. What is it called when a ball is returned immediately after its bounce? (p. 67)
    a. a volley. d. a courtesy stroke.
    b. a drop volley. e. a groundstroke.
    c. a half-volley.
51. Where is "no man's land"? (p. 67)
    a. in the alley on either side of the court.
    b. the forecourt area near the net.
    c. the mid-court area, behind the service line.
    d. the backcourt area near the baseline.
    e. behind the baseline.
52. What term refers to a point that must be replayed? (p. 67)
    a. let. b. fault. c. deuce. d. net ball. e. dead ball.
53. Who competes in Davis Cup matches? (p. 65)
    a. men of all countries.
    b. women of all countries.
    c. men and women of England and the United States.
    d. women of England and the United States.
    e. men and women of the United States only.
54. What is the meaning of the term "ace"? (p. 64)
    a. The server won the point.
    b. The first serve was a good service.
    c. The receiver was unable to return a good service.
    d. The receiver was unable to contact a good service.
55. If your opponent lobs you, what is your return called? (p. 68)
    a. overhand. d. overhand or overhead.
    b. overhead. e. overhead or smash.
    c. smash.

56. What is meant by the term "not up"?   (p. 68)
    a. The ball bounced twice before the player hit it.
    b. The player's racket hit the ground before it hit the ball.
    c. The player missed the ball completely.
    d. The ball hit the net before the player hit it.
    e. The ball landed outside the court boundaries.
57. What does it mean when the TV announcer says, "It's match point!"?   (p. 67)
    a. The next point could complete the match.
    b. If the server wins the next point, he wins the match.
    c. In the deciding set of the match, the score at that particular point is tied in number
        of games won.
    d. The receiver can make a service break if he wins the next point.
58. Which of the following organizations governs the play of tennis in this country?   (p. 75)
    a. United States Tennis Association.
    b. United States Lawn Tennis Association.
    c. American Tennis Association.
    d. American Lawn Tennis Association.
    e. National Public Parks Tennis Association.
59. Which of the following gives correct information concerning stringing?   (pp. 73-74)
    a. Nylon is affected by changes in temperature.
    b. Nylon is comparatively expensive.
    c. Gut is affected by moisture.
    d. Gut has comparatively little elasticity.
60. When a team plays every other team in the tournament, what type of tournament is
    being played?   (p. 69)
    a. single elimination.   d. round robin.
    b. double elimination.   e. consolation.
    c. ladder.

MULTIPLE TRUE AND FALSE

Each of the numbered phrases completes the lettered stem. If the completed statement is true,
place a T on your answer sheet next to the appropriate number; if the completed statement is
false or partially false, place an F next to the appropriate number. Answer T or F for each numbered phrase.
A. When using the forehand grip: (pp. 8-9)
    61. the thumb extends up the top plate of the handle of the racket.
    62. the forefinger is extended directly up the handle of the racket.
    63. the racket face should be at right angles to the ground when the player grips the
         racket.
B. In executing the forehand drive: (pp. 8-12)
    64. the follow-through should be in the direction of the intended ball flight.
    65. the ball should be contacted when it is opposite the right foot.
    66. the player should turn toward the right-hand alley.
    67. a beginner should attempt to play the ball when it is approximately waist high.
C. In executing the backhand drive: (pp. 12-15)
    68. the palm of the racket hand should be facing the ground.
    69. the player should look over his right shoulder at the oncoming ball.
    70. the racket head should lead the arm on the forward swing.
    71. the player should use the forehand grip.
D. In executing a drive, the beginner should: (pp. 11, 12, 14)
    72. stroke the ball on the rise or as soon after the bounce as possible.
    73. look at the spot where he wants to place the ball.
E. In order to insure proper timing, a player should: (pp. 15-16)
    74. start to move into position as the ball bounces.
    75. start the backswing after moving into position.
    76. attempt to get in the direct path of the ball.

F. Which of the following statements contribute to good form in serving?   (pp. 16-19)
  77. The ball should be released from the tossing hand as the racket begins to swing down.
  78. The left side should point toward the intended direction of the serve.
  79. The server's arm and wrist action should be tense.
  80. The ball should be hit with the racket arm fully extended.
  81. The ball should be contacted above and in front of the right shoulder.
  82. The forward swing and follow-through should be downward.
  83. The balls should be held in the palm of the tossing hand.
  84. The player should rotate his trunk and shift his weight forward during the forward swing.
  85. The body should "jackknife" forward during the follow-through.
  86. During the backswing, the racket head should drop behind the head and practically scratch the back.
G. Assuming that your opponent is a good net player, which of the following strokes would you use against him when he is at the net and you are in the backcourt?   (pp. 43-44)
  87. a dropshot hit to either side of the court.
  88. a groundstroke hit directly at him.
  89. a lob hit to his baseline.
  90. a passing shot hit down either sideline.
  91. a short topspin crosscourt.
H. It is considered good strategy to: (pp. 38-40)
  92. vary the pace and placement of your shots.
  93. hit down the middle of the court, thus bisecting the angle with your shot.
  94. use the half-volley as much as possible.
  95. keep your drives low to the net (within one foot), especially when your opponent is in the backcourt.
I. Players should change ends of the court when the score is: (p. 52)
  96. 6-0.
  97. 6-3, 3-4.
  98. 5-7, 6-4, 1-3.
  99. 3-6, 6-1.
J. It is considered good tennis etiquette: (pp. 57-63)
  100. for the server to call the score before serving.
  101. to return balls belonging to another court.
  102. for a spectator to applaud good strokes as they occur during the rally.
  103. to call "good" when your opponent hits the ball in the court.
  104. to complain to your partner about misplaying whenever the point is lost.
  105. to refrain from poaching.
  106. to assist the linejudges in calling the lines.
  107. to accept coaching from your friends when changing ends of the court.
  108. to practice with players of lesser skill occasionally.

TRUE AND FALSE

On your answer sheet, place a T if the statement is true; place an F if the statement is false or partially false.

109. Beginners learning to play tennis should use "heavy" balls rather than light ones.   (p. 5)
110. During a rally, a ball hit before the bounce is called a volley.   (p. 70)
111. The forehand grip is one of the grips recommended for serving.   (p. 16)
112. The same racket face should contact the ball on both the forehand and backhand drives.   (pp. 8-16)
113. In a slice serve, when the face of the racket contacts the ball, the face of the racket is flat.   (pp. 18, 25)

114. The dropshot should *not* be attempted by beginners. (p. 27)
115. Acceptable strategy in doubles calls for one partner to play up near the net and the other partner to play back near the baseline. (p. 41)
116. It is easy to remember from which side of the center mark to serve because an even number of points played means the next serve is from the left-hand side, and an odd number of points played means the next serve is from the right-hand side. (p. 49)
117. The player receiving the serve must stand within the boundaries of the court. (p. 50)
118. In the 9 point sudden death tie-breaker, in order to win the tie-breaker, you have to be ahead by 2 points. (p. 55)
119. Volleyers usually prefer a head-heavy racket while baseline players seem to prefer a handle-heavy racket. (p. 74)
120. The USPTA is an organization of teaching professionals. (p. 70)

Knowledge Test Answer Key

Multiple Choice		Multiple True-False		True-False
1. c	31. d	61. F	85. F	109. T
2. b	32. d	62. F	86. T	110. T
3. c	33. d	63. T	87. F	111. T
4. d	34. d	64. T	88. F	112. F
5. c	35. e	65. F	89. T	113. F
6. d	36. a	66. T	90. T	114. T
7. e	37. d	67. T	91. T	115. F
8. a	38. d	68. T	92. T	116. F
9. d	39. a	69. T	93. F	117. F
10. a	40. d	70. T	94. F	118. F
11. e	41. c	71. F	95. F	119. F
12. b	42. c	72. F	96. F	120. T
13. c	43. d	73. F	97. T	
14. d	44. b	74. F	98. F	
15. a	45. b	75. F	99. T	
16. d	46. d	76. F	100. T	
17. c	47. c	77. F	101. T	
18. b	48. c	78. T	102. F	
19. b	49. c	79. F	103. F	
20. b	50. c	80. T	104. F	
21. d	51. c	81. T	105. F	
22. c	52. a	82. F	106. F	
23. a	53. a	83. F	107. F	
24. a	54. d	84. T	108. T	
25. c	55. e			
26. b	56. a			
27. c	57. a			
28. b	58. a			
29. b	59. c			
30. a	60. d			

Rating System

110 or better:	Smashing! You could be a pro!
100-109:	Well done! You're doing all right.
90-99:	Pretty good—might check out the ones you missed.
80-89:	You must have lost your grip—better read the book (again)!!
79 or less:	Start now, hit the book and get on the ball.

ANSWERS TO EVALUATION QUESTIONS

*Performance answer

| Page | Answer and Page Reference |

1. 4 *

2. 12 *When hitting to backcourt targets, the ball should clear the net by three or four feet. (p. 32)
    When playing from the backcourt, keep your shots deep with medium height and medium speed. (p. 39)

3. 30 C-D. Players are side by side in good net position from which they should be able to control the net. Probably the best attack against such a strong position is to lob over their heads, attempting to force them into the backcourt.
    A-B is a very weak position, subject to attack down either sideline or diagonally between the players. While maintaining parallel position, E and F are too far from the net to hit aggressive volleys and are subject to attack by low shots hit to their feet. (pp. 41-45)

4. 33 *

5. 40 To Y. The net is lower in the center than at the sideline and the court is longer when hitting to the deep crosscourt corner. You therefore have greater margin for error and more time to get back to your position. Note that in the diagram, the dotted lines bisect the angle of possible return, both from point Z and from point Y. Hitting to Y provides the shortest distance for you to recover to a sound position that bisects the angle of your opponent's possible return. (p. 40)

6. 45 In the right service court, No. 2 or No. 4, and in the left court, No. 7 or No. 9 The choice depends on your opponent; force him to return the ball with his weakest stroke. Occasionally serve directly at opponent, No. 3 and No. 8. A slice serve to No. 1 forces receiver out of position most. By serving to No. 4 or No. 7, the server has automatically "bisected the angle." (p. 41)

7. 53 The score is love-15; 30-love; 40-15; 40-30; 15 all; deuce, advantage server; deuce; advantage receiver; game receiver. (pp. 51-52)

8. 54 *

9. 59 *

10. 63 *

Index